THE CIA FILES

CENTRAL INTELLIGENCE AGENCY

The CIA's task is twofold: to coordinate the intelligence efforts of the U.S. government, and to collect, evaluate, analyze, produce, and disseminate foreign intelligence. Since its foundation, the CIA has provided and continues to provide the most accurate, comprehensive, and objective information available about national security matters.

The CIA has a limited number of positions available for applicants with backgrounds in computer science; electrical engineering; Asian, Slavic and Middle Eastern languages; economics; and international relations.

Positions are open to U.S. citizens of all ethnic and cultural backgrounds. Salaries are competitive. Successful completion of medical and psychological evaluations, a polygraph interview, and an extensive background investigation are required.

OUR BUSINESS IS KNOWING THE WORLD'S BUSINESS.

above *Join the CIA—a recruitment ad in a campus magazine,* Hispanic Almanac *(courtesy of* Parascope*).*

THE CIA FILES

SECRETS OF "THE COMPANY"

MICK FARREN

consultant:
MICHAEL SIMMONS

Foreword by Charles Rappleye

CLB

CONTENTS

Dedication
This book is dedicated to . . . but I wouldn't want to mention their names

5112: The CIA Files
Published 1999 by
CLB, an imprint of
Quadrillion Publishing Limited,
Godalming Business Centre,
Woolsack Way, Godalming,
GU7 1XW, England.
Distributed in the US by
Quadrillion Publishing Inc.,
230 Fifth Avenue, New York,
NY 10001

copyright © 1999
Quadrillion Publishing Limited

ISBN 1-84100-139-2

Printed and bound in Italy by
New Interlitho Italia SpA

8

Foreword
11

1
THE COMPANY
An Introduction and Brief History
12

America's first spies
"Wild Bill" Donovan and the OSS
Guatemala, 1952
The CIA tackles Cuba
The Bay of Pigs fiasco
Kennedy moves closer to Cuba
The Phoenix Program
The PSYOPS campaign
Air America

2
THE SHADOW GOVERNMENT
Who's in Charge Here?
38

The founding of the CIA
Influence abroad: Teheran, 1953
Stansfield Turner: an attempt at morality
Moving into FBI territory
COINTELPRO and CHAOS
The secrets of Mount Weather
The currency of drugs
Tony (Poe) Posmepny
Oliver North and the Contras
Clinton and the CIA
The trouble with Afghanistan

★
9

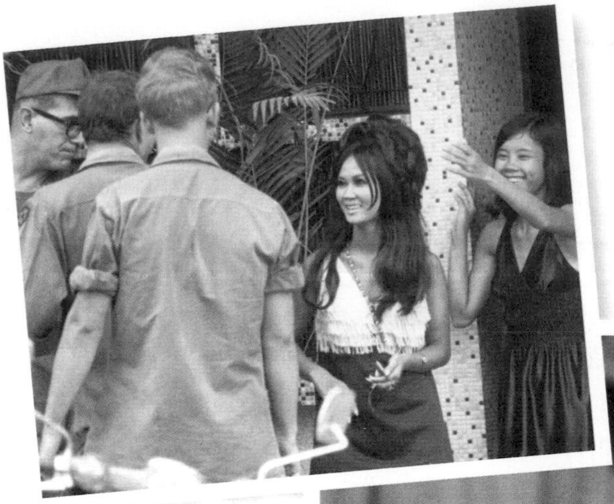

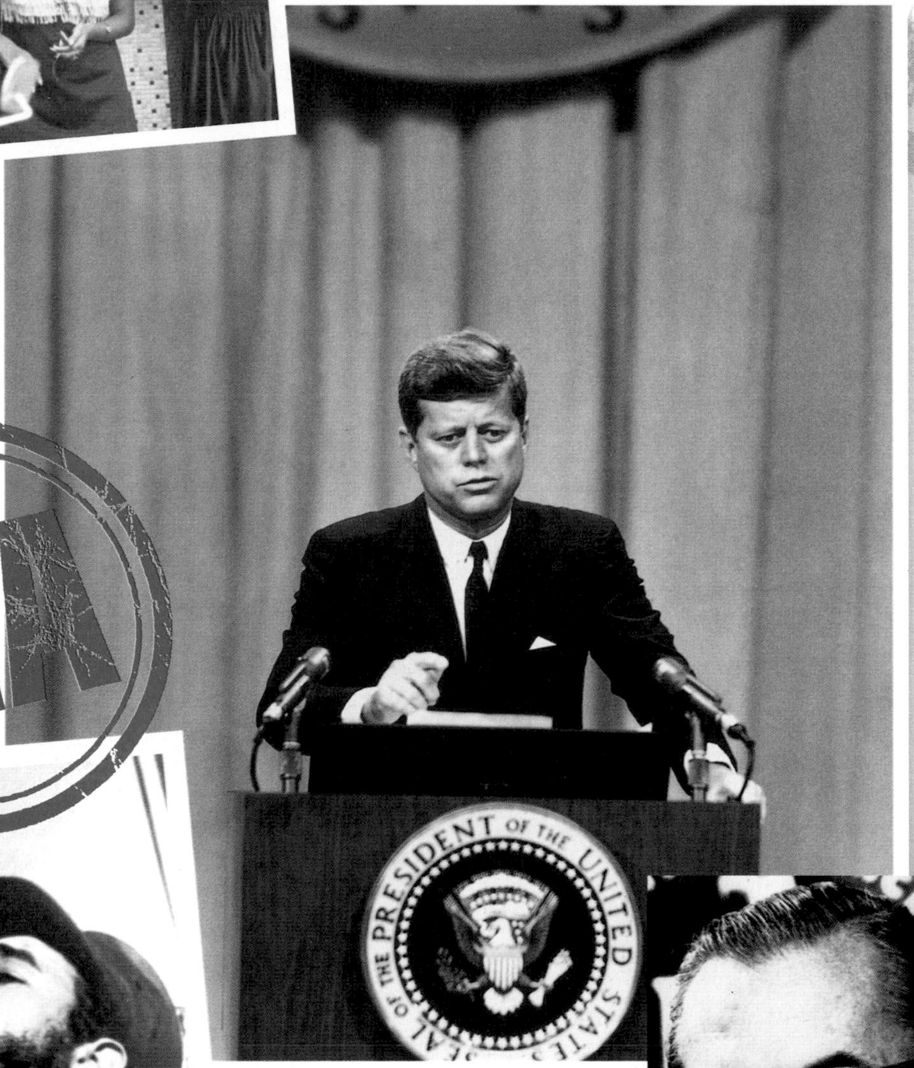
SEAL OF THE PRESIDENT OF THE UNITED STATES

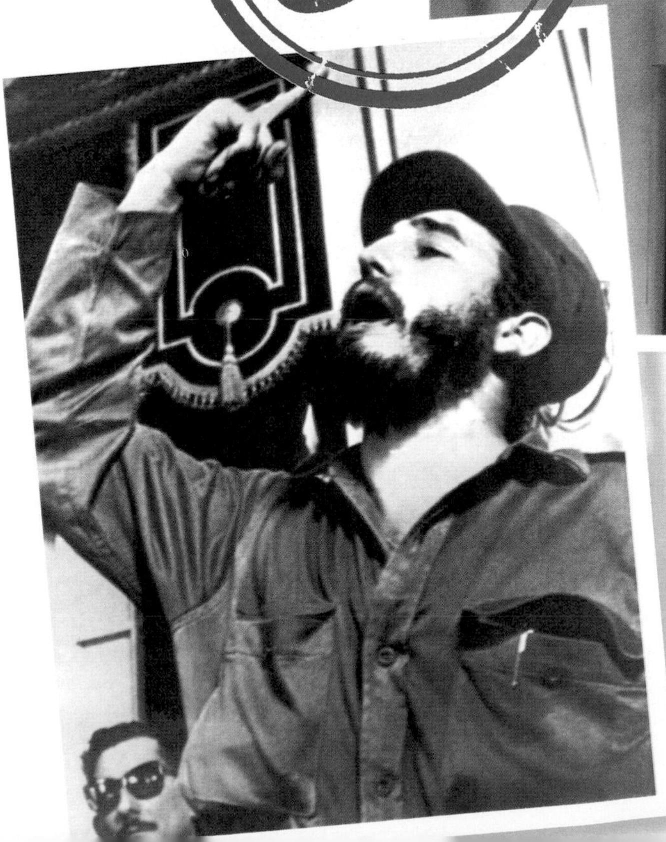

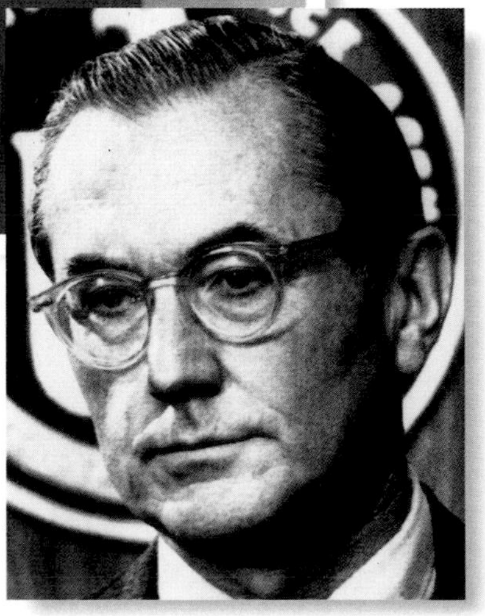

FOREWORD

Inside the Agency they called them the Family Jewels, a top secret list of the CIA's most offensive illegal operations, including assassination and mind control, that surfaced in censored form only after an aggressive probe by the US Senate.

It was a misnomer. They should have been dubbed Family Secrets, for they were the equivalent, in the US body politic, of the skeletons that lurk in the dark recesses of our collective experience—incest, rape, torture, murder. The CIA has become a popular icon for government misdeeds, but even such popular fictions as "The X-Files" can only begin to approximate to the fearful reality of the Agency's 50-year tour of the dark side.

It's a virtual catalogue of perfidy, as if, cloaked in secrecy and shielded by the presumption of national interest, the plotters at the Agency determined at the outset to explore the depths of the far reaches of evil. The schemes would be comic if they were not so grim. There was murder, of course, but not just simple execution—wholesale slaughter, systematic torture and the targeting of some of the world's most popular, most charismatic leaders. There was nefarious experimentation with dangerous drugs and large-scale experiments at mind control—often with unwitting subjects, and often with dire consequences. There was drug trafficking on a scale that destabilized entire nations—including the US itself. And those are just the projects we know about. Remember, secrecy and obfuscation are central to the Agency's mission. The true extent of the CIA's misdeeds can only be extrapolated.

Of course, the Agency doesn't always achieve its goals. Indeed, in Iran at the fall of the Shah, or in India with its shocking nuclear tests, the CIA was taken completely unawares. But delving into the hidden history of the CIA is more than simply an excursion into the lurid. It's an exercise to help expand the bounds of credulity, a corrective to the bland notions of peaceable goodwill issued by Uncle Sam's propagandists—exactly the sort of pabulum that serves as cover for the Agency's tricksters. Read on, and remember—a healthy dose of paranoia may be your best chance to grasp what's really going on.

CHARLES RAPPLEYE

CHAPTER ONE

THE COMPANY

An Introduction and Brief History

When the United States entered World War Two in the wake of the Japanese attack on Pearl Harbor, it had the manpower and the vast industrial base to fight and win a global conflict. In the area of a workable intelligence network, however, it was sadly lacking, with nothing like the capabilities of either its allies or its enemies. The British had been playing the spy/counter-spy game for almost 400 years, since the time of the Spanish Armada, when Sir Francis Walsingham created one of the most efficient espionage operations in Europe. In France, first Cardinal Richelieu and then Napoleon had raised intelligence gathering to a fine art. The Russians had been going about the business of international spying since the reign of Peter the Great, and, when Germany was united under Bismarck in the late 19th century, the Iron Chancellor had made sure that it inherited all of the espionage know-how of Prussian militarism. For centuries, the Europeans had been playing what came to be known as "the Great Game," in which rival imperial powers jockeyed for power and position all the way from London, Paris, Berlin, and Moscow to the furthest flung outposts of each respective empire.

★
13

facing page *Players in the Company's "Great Game" (clockwise from top left): Josef Mengele, the Nazi "Angel of Death," who was protected by the CIA; Allen Dulles, who ran it during the 1950s Cold War; William Colby, who ran its covert operations in Vietnam; and John F. Kennedy, who swore to dismantle it.*

above *Allan Pinkerton, Abraham Lincoln's spymaster during the Civil War and the founder of the Pinkerton Detective Agency. He also investigated the Lincoln assassination.*

right *During the Civil War, intelligence was a disorganized and amateurish affair, and much hard intelligence was only gathered by cavalry units in the field and spies who were distrusted by commanders on both sides.*

right *The attack on Pearl Harbor forced the USA to take its intelligence capabilities seriously, and triggered the formation of the Office of Strategic Services (OSS).*

below *"Wild Bill" Donovan, who headed the World War Two OSS and created many of the organizational patterns that would shape the early CIA.*

America's first spies

In America, during the 19th and even the early 20th centuries, the situation was very different. On a continent of pioneers, settlers, and immigrants, that was still pushing its way west into a largely unknown interior, the USA had needed scouts rather than spies. Even during the Civil War, intelligence had been a wildly disorganized and highly amateurish affair. The Confederacy had relied on a collection of Southern gentlemen-adventurers and femmes fatales. The Union had been somewhat more efficient, in so far as Abraham Lincoln had appointed Allan Pinkerton to oversee the Northern spy net. Unfortunately, after hostilities ceased, instead of making the operation a part of the Federal Secret Service, Pinkerton went on to commercialize what he had created in the form of the Pinkerton Detective Agency. In its later, overseas, adventures in Cuba and the Philippines, America had little need for sophisticated intelligence work—more, the cowboy courage of Teddy Roosevelt's Rough Riders—and the US had entered World War One so late, and in such a

largely symbolic role, that it had virtually no contact with the more covert areas of the conflict.

Matters would remain virtually unchanged until 1941, when the reality of war with Japan and Germany would force the United States to completely reevaluate its intelligence capabilities. Although there is some indication that US Naval Intelligence may have had some clues as to the Japanese plans for the air assault on Pearl Harbor, and may have even warned President Franklin Roosevelt of the impending disaster, the near destruction of its Pacific fleet left America convinced that, as a nation, it was dangerously vulnerable.

"Wild Bill" Donovan and the OSS

The need was clearly for a crash course in the intricacies of the spy game, and no one was more aware of this than the President himself, who immediately set the wheels in motion to create what would, by 1942, become the Office of Strategic Services—the OSS—and the immediate forerunner of the Central Intelligence Agency.

To head up the new OSS, Roosevelt selected General William Donovan, a hero of World War One who had already been a military advisor to the President even before the Japanese attack. Burly and dauntlessly energetic, "Wild Bill" Donovan was a millionaire Republican, educated at Columbia Law School, and very much a part of the East Coast establishment. After serving in France, he had returned to civilian life and a partnership in a Wall Street law firm. Even though a political opponent of Franklin Roosevelt's New Deal, Donovan enjoyed Roosevelt's trust, friendship, and—most crucial of all—direct access to the inner sanctums of the White House.

"Wild Bill" Donovan's jovial, outgoing personality and his upperclass social background played a considerable part in setting the overall tone and style of the agency that he was creating. It was a tone and style that would outlive the OSS and do a great deal to shape the actions and attitudes of its successor, the CIA. As he began to recruit the potential agents and controllers who would form the backbone of his brand new spy network, he deliberately selected individuals who were, for the most part, simply younger versions of himself. To some extent this was Donovan borrowing from the methods of the British MI5 and MI6, in which the hierarchy were sons of the upper class who could combine perfect manners and

THE USA HAD NEEDED SCOUTS RATHER THAN SPIES

exquisite taste with a brutal ruthlessness—the models that, in fiction, Ian Fleming used when he first created James Bond.

While the British recruited their operatives at Oxford and Cambridge and on the playing fields of Eton, Donovan looked to the Harvard, Yale, and the other Ivy League Colleges of the American East Coast. His ideal agent profile was a football hero with a talent for languages and lateral thinking who wasn't afraid to mix it up if the game got dirty. Indeed, Donovan was so successful in his efforts that the OSS gained enough of a reputation for elitism that the other armed services dubbed it the "Oh So Social." He particularly looked for two qualities that would, over the years, as the OSS grew into the CIA as we know it today, prove to be a double-edged sword. The first was a definite tendency for his potential agents to see themselves as a cut above the common herd and not feel bound by the legal or moral restraints of lesser mortals. The other was the ability to carry out their assignments without question or any need for detailed explanations. One of the earliest catch phrases

SECRET SOCIETIES

"Wild Bill" Donovan's recruitment policy of signing up socially connected young men from Ivy League colleges, and the way that virtually the same class-conscious system was maintained by the CIA, gave birth to some strange and constantly circulating paranoia that may have a thin basis in truth, or could just as easily be a piece of conspiracy folklore. The CIA's combination of class and cult-like secrecy has, over the years, generated a wave of speculation that it is affiliated with, or even controlled by, semi-legendary secret societies like the Harvard Skull and Bones Club, the Yale Scroll and Key, and from them through to the Freemasons, the Knights Templar, the Trilateral Commission, and, if the imagination is sufficiently fevered, the New World Order and aliens from outer space. Of course, the very same people who make these claims will also attempt to prove that the US government is controlled by the Bavarian Illuminati by showing you the eye in the pyramid on the one dollar bill.

Joking and paranoia aside, however, the fact that such bizarre rumors could gather around the primary counter-intelligence agency of the most powerful country in the world would indicate that, at the very least, the CIA has suffered for a long time from a serious public relations and image problem.

of the fledgling OSS—"to reason is treason"—has, in hindsight, a very ominous ring to it.

Although the OSS had its share of high adventure and covert operations—celebrated in a number of movies, including *OSS*, starring Alan Ladd, and also a 1950s TV series of the same name by far the bulk of its work was the routine, deskbound grind of collating and analyzing the mountains of data that are generated by any combat situation. It also ran a highly efficient scientific research section, with the primary task of perfecting small and easily concealed weapons for the various resistance and partisan organizations fighting in the occupied countries in both Europe and the Far East.

The development of these often ingenious devices was one of Donovan's favorite projects within the OSS. It seemed to appeal to his sense of humor and he gave it a great deal of his personal attention. Shortly after the US declared war, he issued a directive to his newly recruited scientists: "I need every subtle device and every underhand trick to use against the Germans and Japanese—by our own people—but especially by the underground resistance programs in all the occupied countries. You have to invent

"HERE'S A CHANCE TO RAISE MERRY HELL"

them. Throw all your normal, law abiding concepts out of the window. Here's a chance to raise merry hell."

Among the products of this "raising merry hell" was an explosive named "Aunt Jemima." Created by an OSS Harvard-trained chemist, Dr. George Kistiakowsky, the flour-like chemical looked and tasted like pancake mix and could even be safely baked and eaten, but when fitted with a detonator, could produce a blast similar in power to dynamite and was used extensively against the Japanese in China to blow up bridges and destroy railway tracks. Another weapon, codenamed "Who Me?," worked on a whole different level. As a colorless form of skatole liquid that smelled like an intense approximation of diarrhea, it was secretly distributed to children in occupied cities who were encouraged to spray it on enemy officers in crowded streets.

Like the CIA, however, the OSS also had its darker side. It planned a number of assassination attempts against Adolf Hitler and was almost certainly in touch with the German officers whose 1944 bomb plot came within a whisker of blowing up the Führer at his "Wolf's Lair"

left *Adolf Hitler; the OSS prepared a number of psychological profiles of the Nazi leader and also made plans to assassinate him.*

★
16
=

right *J. Edgar Hoover; the FBI director initially opposed the establishment of the CIA, fearing it might cut into his power.*

far right *CIA Director Allen Dulles.*

below *The CIA official seal.*

headquarters. Other conspiracies may have been directed at targets closer to home. Although no hard evidence has ever been unearthed, rumors continue to circulate that somehow Donovan and the OSS, possibly at the behest of President Harry Truman, had a hand in rigging the car accident that killed General George Patton.

Following the Nazi surrender, Patton had become something of an embarrassment. He had made repeated public statements to the effect that the war with Germany was only a prologue to the real conflict, the one with unholy communism, and that the Soviet Union, far from being a victorious ally, was the true enemy. He had even gone so far as advocate the rearming of certain divisions of the SS to be ready to fight the Russians when the time came. The fear in Washington was that Patton would take the law into his own hands and use the tanks of his battlehardened Third Army to spark some incident that would then flare into an unstoppable and all out war with the Soviets. Certainly a convenient automobile accident would prove less embarrassing than the public dismissal of a man who was, to many, a national hero.

While World War Two continued to rage, the attitude of "anything goes" was totally acceptable, but with the collapse of Japan and Germany, matters became less clear-cut. Patton was far from alone in believing that communism was the real foe, and although the Truman administration didn't share the desire of "Old Blood and Guts" for an immediate headlong rush into World War Three, the alliance against Nazism was quickly divided by what Winston Churchill called "the Iron Curtain." Although the actual battle wasn't engaged, the battle lines were clearly drawn. When, in 1947, the US Congress passed a National Security Act that absorbed the OSS into the newly created Central Intelligence Agency, the new agency's officially stated assignment was to "coordinate, evaluate, and disseminate intelligence from other US agencies and to advise the President and National Security Council." An unwritten subtext, however, to this seemingly bureaucratic agenda was that the CIA was, in reality, charged with fighting the Cold War against communism. Not that it had a totally free hand, though. A determined move, led by FBI Director J. Edgar Hoover, was made to limit the powers of the CIA, especially in the area of domestic intelligence operations. The Agency was prohibited from operating inside the United States itself, and it had no "police, subpoena, or law enforcement powers or internal security functions." Over and above the coordination of data, CIA operations were to be carried out strictly overseas. The Agency code with regard to foreigners was largely unfettered, but when it came to spying on US citizens in their homes and at their jobs, that was totally the province of the FBI and the local and state police.

These were the rules, but from the very start, and certainly when Allen Dulles took control in 1953 and greatly enlarged the Agency, the prevailing attitude was that rules were only made to be broken. The CIA was all that stood between America and the godless Red hordes

right *Inmates of Nazi concentration camps were subjected to horrific medical experiments, the records of which would later be obtained by the OSS as part of the notorious Operation Paperclip.*

below *Dr. Josef Mengele, the head of "medical research" at Auschwitz.*

AN EXTRAORDINARY PICTURE FROM THE NOTORIOUS CONCENTRATION CAMP AT DACHAU, NEAR MUNICH, WHICH APPEARED IN THE "ILLUSTRIERTE BEOBACHTER" (PUBLISHED BY HITLER'S OWN PUBLISHING FIRM) OVER THE CAPTION:-

"A GROUP OF POLITICAL REPEATERS - PERSONS WHO WOULD NOT STOP THEIR AGITATION AND SUBVERSIVE ACTIVITY AGAINST THE STATE EVEN AFTER A PREVIOUS IMPRISONMENT.

...ly a very large number of political ...ds branded as 'anti-social elements', ...re Jews, Communists, Socialists, ...ergymen, profiteers, 'unsocial' ...men who spend their weekly wages in ...e failed to display proper support ...rprises, such as the individual who ...National Socialist Winter Relief ...nd".

...ration camps are held at the ...

and if anyone questioned the Agency's methods, all answers could be refused on the grounds of national security. It was an attitude that would make the Agency a near law unto itself for almost six decades and one that, to some degree, continues today, even though in recent years the CIA has come under increasing scrutiny and many of its dirtier little secrets have been given public airing.

Almost from the very start, the CIA seemed to develop an increasingly odd perspective of what might be justified in the thwarting of communism. Even the OSS under Donovan had made some moves that appeared to indicate, although it was now peacetime, that the organization would continue to "throw all normal, law-abiding concepts out of the window." As the Nazis collapsed, the Russians and Americans found themselves in a furious race for German technology and military secrets. While other branches of military intelligence were scrambling to round up all the

rocket scientists, aeronautical engineers and advanced weapon specialists they could find, the OSS, under the codename "Operation Paperclip," went after the operatives and records of Nazi intelligence from what was left of the Abwehr, the SS, and the Gestapo. Since they were also charged to search out Nazi war criminals and bring them to justice, a grimly ironic situation began to develop in which one set of OSS agents might be protecting or even have recruited a notorious Nazi like Klaus Barbie, the Gestapo "Butcher of Lyons," while their colleagues were conducting an intensive manhunt for him.

The OSS not only had a number of key surviving Nazis, but they also had their files and records. One OSS team, shifting through the paperwork that had been left behind at Dachau concentration camp, discovered the horrific detailed reports of the barbaric medical experiments that had been conducted on the SS's prisoner guinea pigs. The Nazi doctors had literally tested human beings to the absolute limits of endurance and painstakingly noted the results. All of this monstrous data went into the files of the OSS, was inherited by the CIA and, to this day, much of it,

IF YOU'VE MADE ONE DEAL WITH THE DEVIL, ALL THE OTHERS BECOME A WHOLE LOT SIMPLER

left *A German V2 rocket is launched at a target in Southern England, and a new era in warfare begins*

in particular the information dealing with mind control and psychoactive drugs, has never been made public. Even though their shocking data lived on, the Nazi doctors were, at least, tried and convicted at the second round of Nuremberg war crimes trials. Of the sixteen accused, seven were sentenced to death and nine to long prison terms. Other wanted Nazis, though, were far luckier.

Definite indications exist that first the OSS and then the CIA, if not actively giving assistance, turned an exceedingly blind eye to Odessa and other organizations dedicated to spiriting prominent Nazis away to Canada, the USA, and South and Central America. They also took very little notice and certainly never questioned the roles played by the regimes of Juan Peron in Argentina and Alfredo Stroessner in Paraguay in establishing sanctuary for war criminals like Josef Mengele, the doctor in charge of the Nazi human experiments, and Adolf Eichmann, the SS officer who implemented the "final solution," the Nazi extermination program.

On the principle that, if you've made one deal with the devil, all others become a whole lot simpler, once the CIA had compromised itself by doing business with what was left of the Nazi hierarchy, cozying up to various right-wing dictatorships or international drug cartels seems to have posed no real moral problem. In the same way, but a lot closer to home, the Agency had few qualms about enlisting the aid of the most powerful organized crime families when the need arose. Although one can't equate the crimes of the Mob with the atrocities of the Nazis, they still weren't suitable bedfellows for a branch of the United States government. The CIA rapidly appeared to be developing a policy that, if you were against communism, then nothing else really mattered. More than any other factor, it was this bizarre single-mindedness of attitude and the unholy alliances it created that not only brought the Agency into general disrepute, but also produced some catastrophic situations that will go on reverberating well into the next century. All down the line, the question is begged. How long can a supposedly democratically sanctioned organization go on doing business with the likes of thugs, madmen, and gangsters without, to some degree, starting to resemble them? The CIA had apparently forgotten the often

THE FRENCH CONNECTION

Almost as soon as it was created, the CIA became enmeshed in the shadowy world of international narcotics traffic. In 1947 the French were fighting a guerrilla war in Indochina against the Viet Minh, the forerunners of the Viet Cong, with the total support of the USA and the Truman administration. In protest against the war, the 80,000-strong communist-controlled dockworkers union in the French port of Marseilles were boycotting all ships carrying supplies to the war. It fell to the CIA to do what they could to terminate this boycott. The situation obviously required a team of efficient strike breakers, hard-bitten and ruthless enough to go up against the union men, themselves no strangers to breaking heads. Indeed, many of the dockers were ex-World War Two resistance fighters. The most suitable candidates for the job turned out to be the

Corsican Guerini brothers, heads of the most powerful crime family in the city.

The Guerinis and their boys went to work with gusto and, by the end of the year, the boycott was history. At that point they approached the CIA looking for their final payoff. Their demand was simple. They wanted a monopoly— untroubled by law enforcement—on importing opium from South East Asia, processing it into heroin, and then shipping it onto organized crime in New York and other US cities. A grateful Agency was only too eager to agree. It seemed a more than fair arrangement in the global war on communism. Freedom, the Agency reasoned, doesn't come without a price. The arrangement between the CIA and the Guerinis would survive intact for almost a quarter of a century.

repeated quote of philosopher Friedrich Nietzsche—"he who fights with monsters might take care lest he thereby becomes a monster."

For the CIA, the war against communism truly got under way when Allen Dulles became its director in 1953. Allen Dulles and his brother, John Foster Dulles, the Secretary of State, were both rabid anti-communists, supporters of big business, and, between them, they controlled American foreign policy throughout the 1950s and left a legacy that lingered for at least another ten years after that. To the Dulles brothers, foreign policy meant stopping communism at any cost, and with as little consultation as possible with the generally acquiescent President Dwight Eisenhower. It was the Dulles brothers who really invented the doctrine of "what the President doesn't know can't hurt him politically," and set the precedent for the CIA going its own merry, secretive way,

as though it wasn't responsible to anyone or anything. It was on Dulles' watch that the Agency started to be called the "Company," and see itself as a quasi-independent corporate entity who's primary business was knowing what was best for America, the world, and even humanity itself.

In one respect, Allen Dulles was eminently well equipped to head up the CIA. Both he and his brother had, before going into government, been high-powered corporate lawyers with a reputation for ruthlessness. He had at one point been a director of the J. Henry Schroder Banking Corporation and, from the time he took over at the CIA, the Schroder Bank would have an exclusive on laundering funds for the Agency's covert operations.

In the 1940s, CIA direct action had been mainly a matter of fine tuning, but in the aftermath of the Korean War, Allen Dulles, with the greater manpower and economic resources that he brought with him, endowed the

right *A large bag of cocaine with a street value of some hundreds of thousands of dollars. Even as early as 1947 the CIA was drawn into involvement with the drug trade.*

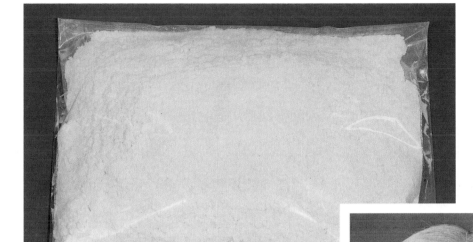

below *John Foster Dulles, the US Secretary of State during the Eisenhower administration. With his brother Allen, Dulles would shape America's Cold War game plan.*

21

Agency with a capability for full-scale, paramilitary operations. No longer content with just bringing pressure and money to bear in foreign elections, Dulles was preparing the Agency to target entire countries for various kinds of destabilization leading to revolution or military coups, with the CIA supplying advisors, finances, and weapons at every step of the way. If a nation's government didn't conform to Dulles' view of what might be in the United States' best interest, he had no qualms about simply removing it.

Guatemala, 1952

A textbook example of bringing down a government is the case of the CIA-sponsored revolution in Guatemala. In 1952, the Guatemalan President, a left-leaning, ex-colonel called Jacobo Arbenz, signed into law a land reform decree that would have effectively nationalized the vast plantations of the US-owned United Fruit Company. Arbenz had also strengthened the labor unions, particularly those of the agriculture workers, and, since United Fruit owned the lion's share of the Guatemalan agribusiness, its American directors found themselves facing wage demands and strike threats. As if all this wasn't bad enough, the Guatemalan Communist Party was a small but crucial minority in the country's parliament and often gave much needed support to the radical President. Clearly, Arbenz

was exactly the kind of individual the Dulles brothers didn't want holding power in Central America. He had to go, and he had to go quickly before other folks south of the border also started talking land reform and demanding a living wage.

The Dulles' decision to remove Arbenz, however, wasn't entirely a matter of politics. Money also insinuated its way into the picture. The Schroder Bank, Dulles' former employer, owned a large slice of the Guatemalan railroads, while a number of prominently placed members of the Eisenhower administration had serious financial interests in United Fruit. Ideology went hand in hand with vested interests and the Dulles' proved themselves to be in total agreement with Henry Ford's time-honored declaration that "what was good for business was, by definition, good for the USA."

The ousting of Arbenz was given the codename "Operation Success" and the first salvos were fired in the propaganda arena. All across Latin America, the CIA planted articles and news stories, both in print and on radio, and even handed out leaflets and comic books that all attempted to spread the alarmist impression that Guatemala was going to fall to the communists at any moment. Rumors were spread through an already nervous population that Arbenz planned to disband the regular army, set up armed "people's militias" in its place, and make himself the country's absolute dictator. The CIA, working with United Fruit, actually managed to spark a brief armed uprising in the provincial capital of Salama, but this was quickly put down. In charge of this phase of Operation Success was a CIA agent called E. Howard Hunt, who would surface 20 years later as one of Nixon's Watergate burglars.

After the failure of the rising at Salama, the CIA began to crank up the pressure. They chose another ex-colonel, Castillo Armas, to lead an anti-Arbenz "Liberation Army" and set up a "government in exile." Regular diplomats were replaced by CIA agents in the US embassy. Political differences between officers in the Guatemalan armed forces were magnified and exploited. The CIA-controlled

TWO WEEKS LATER THE CIA DROPPED THE BOMB

radio station, La Voz de Liberacion, broadcasting out of Honduras, began giving the impression that thousands of anti-communist freedom fighters were massing on the border, poised to invade, when, in fact, Armas never had more than 400 men under his command at any one time during the entire "revolution." On June 2nd, 1954, an attempt on Arbenz's life was foiled and arrests were made, but he started to lose the support of the army and air force. Two weeks later the CIA quite literally dropped the bomb. Mercenary pilots flew B26 raids over Guatemala, and the CIA radio station broadcast phony recordings, prepared in advance, that purported to be "live" reports of the massive liberation army moving in from Honduras.

At first, Arbenz and his loyal officers stood firm. The tiny invasion force was easily contained and Arbenz appealed to the United Nations, but his pleas for a UN intervention were blocked by US Ambassador Henry Cabot Lodge. Then Dulles administered the coup de grâce. The

left A crucial CIA tactic in Guatemala was to drive a wedge of distrust between President Arbenz and the army.

★
23
=

CIA planes went back into action, bombing and strafing the major cities, including the capital, Guatemala City, and creating havoc in an already dangerously confused situation. At this point Arbenz and his supporters seemed to have cracked. A group of senior officers forced his resignation. Armas and his ragtag "army" entered the capital and, with the support of the CIA, took political control. The removal of Jacobo Arbenz was all over apart from the propaganda wrap-up. Guatemala had been made safe for United Fruit and it would become one of the most troubled and repressive states in all of Latin America. It would also become a CIA staging area and training ground for other operations in Central and South America.

The CIA tackles Cuba

If the overthrow of Arbenz was a CIA dream come true, the situation in Cuba a few years later could well qualify as the Company's worst nightmare. Even Allen Dulles couldn't pretend that Cuba, under the rule of one-time army sergeant, Fulgencio Batista, was anything but a scandalous mess. US corporations ran the sugar plantations, US organized crime ran the resorts and casinos, corruption was endemic, and bribery was a way of life. Cuba was so far gone that not even the CIA could go on propping up Batista and retain any semblance of credibility. That

right *January 1960; a triumphant Fidel Castro rides into Havana at the head of a revolutionary army.*

Batista would ultimately be overthrown by one revolutionary group or another was pretty much a foregone conclusion; that the person to do it should turn out to be Fidel Castro, and his bearded guerrillas from the forests of the Sierra Maestra, came as something of a surprise. However, surprise rapidly turned first to shock and then to fury as it was revealed that the new leader of Cuba, if not an out-and-out communist, certainly embraced a highly radical and dangerous form of socialism. As the banks, the sugar industry, and other American interests were either frozen, seized, or nationalized, the cry went up that Castro had to go.

It was in Cuba that the CIA under Dulles betrayed one of its most vulnerable weaknesses. Ever since the time of "Wild Bill" Donovan, the Company had looked on itself as an elite, a cut above the common herd. It tended to deal with the wealthy, the powerful, and the connected, seeing the poor, the workers, and indigenous populations, as little more than cannon fodder—at best, merely pawns in the game. Unlike British intelligence, the Company was an organization that had little tolerance for mavericks. It wouldn't have had time for strange individualists like

T.E. Lawrence, Orde Wingate, or Sir Richard Burton, unorthodox adventurers who were quite prepared to go native, to vanish into the jungle, or squat in the marketplace disguised as a beggar, if that was what was required to obtain an accurate and clear picture of a situation. The average CIA agent was far more comfortable in the refinement of an embassy, a presidential palace, or sitting at the bar in a five-star hotel, than in the marketplace or a peasant hut, a preference that equipped them poorly, to say the least, for the task of gathering real grassroots information or assessing levels of popular feeling. Time and again, in the Middle East, in Indochina, and in Central America, they made disastrous miscalculations that repeatedly left the US completely unprepared for various violent upheavals. The CIA completely failed to predict the fall of the Shah of Iran and didn't see the collapse of the Soviet Union until it was right on top of them.

To put it bluntly, the CIA frequently had too high an opinion of itself to get down with the mass of the people and find out what was really going on. Under Dulles this was compounded by the fact that the Company was playing an increasingly proactive role, preferring to move and shake, as in Guatemala, rather than remain quiet and merely observe. The first mistake they made with Fidel Castro was to believe that he could never achieve his revolutionary objectives without the direct support of a superpower supplying him with weapons and finance. Since the Company's best information was that Castro and his few hundred men were neither being supported by the USA nor the Soviets, operatives in Havana kept reporting to CIA headquarters in Langley, Virginia, that Castro was doomed to failure. The dismissal of Castro and his guerrillas as little more than poorly armed beatniks continued even after *New York Times* reporter Herbert Matthews had trekked into the mountains to interview Castro and published a front page report with the headline "Batista's Days Are Numbered." After he had come to power, the CIA still took the position that the Castro regime was nothing more than a house of cards. He had little real popular support, it was felt, and one good kick would bring him tumbling down. The kick they decided on turned out to be the Bay of Pigs, and it has to rank as one of the Agency's most humiliating defeats.

The responsibility for removing Castro was designated by Allen Dulles to Richard Bissell, his Director of Covert Operations. The initial scheme was for a simple assassination. A hit on Fidel, Bissell reasoned would not only be quick and clean but also highly cost effective, but as the

CASTRO'S ARMY: LITTLE MORE THAN POORLY ARMED BEATNIKS

methods of removing the Cuban "Commandante" were investigated, they began to verge on something from *Mad* magazine.

Cute as some of the assassination plans might have been, Dulles and Bissell started to lean toward a more direct military strategy. As Castro formed closer ties with the Eastern bloc and started accepting more and more aid from the Soviets, the CIA finally began to take him seriously. He rapidly became the threat the USA had always feared. The Castro government could all too easily—and as it eventually would for a brief period—play host to a possible enemy's nuclear weapon just 90 miles from Miami. Where once Dulles and Bissell might have envisioned a phony invasion to topple Castro, similar to Operation Success in Guatemala, they now began to believe that it might take an offensive that packed considerably more muscle.

The simple answer might have been to send in the marines, but the Dulles brothers were well aware that such direct aggression on the part of the United States against a sovereign nation, no matter how unpopular its leaders, would never be tolerated by either the

right *Castro quickly became the CIA's prime target for destabilization and assassination.*

"WHACK THE BEARD!"

Only in recent years, with the publication of the Inspector General's Report On Plots To Assassinate Fidel Castro released publicly as part of the CIA's Historical Review Program, did it become clear just how intent the Agency was to remove the Cuban leader, but also how inept they were in their efforts. Initially, the idea wasn't to kill Castro. In the early days, it seemed enough either to humiliate or discredit him. Plans were made for various attacks with depilatory chemicals that would make his trademark beard fall out, and cause him to appear totally ridiculous. When, in the early 1960s, Castro was booked to appear on TV on *The David Suskind Show*, the idea was to dust his hotel room with the chemical thallium, a powerful hair removal agent. Fortunately for Fidel, his spot on the show was cancelled and the attempt on his beard never took place.

A second set of schemes were intended to make him seemingly go mad in public. One idea was, by means of an aerosol disguised as an air freshener, to spray a psychoactive chemical similar to lysergic acid (LSD) into the radio station studio used by Castro to broadcast to the Cuban people and make him become incoherent live on the air. Another was to contaminate a box of his favorite cigars with the same drug.

Working with the Mafia

As the CIA began to perceive Castro as more dangerous, however, the pranks accelerated to full-scale plans for his murder. Castro was given the official codename AMTHUG but, unofficially, he was simply referred to as "the Beard." One of the first ideas for killing "the Beard" was to use the Company's mob connections to arrange a Mafia-style shooting. This wasn't to happen, though. Chicago mob boss Sam Giancana vetoed the idea. His men wouldn't let themselves be involved in an attack where the odds against shooters getting away were so slim that it virtually amounted to a suicide mission. They declined to "whack the Beard." Ex-casino boss Joe Trafficante figured he could get an assassin close enough to Castro to poison him, providing the CIA Technical Services Department could come up with a suitably slow-acting chemical that would allow plenty of time for a clean getaway. Working with botulinus toxins, TSD's Dr. Edward Gunn came up with a pill that would make Castro fatally ill, but only after a matter of hours—what Gunn described as "a bacterial mickey." All seemed well until a last-minute test revealed that the deadly pills dissolved so slowly in water that they were easily detectable, and the plan was shelved.

It was from this point on that the plans to kill Castro became decidedly bizarre. The team, headed by Desmond Fitzgerald, still working on an assassination even after JFK had ordered attempts on Castro's life to cease, centered on Fidel's love of scuba diving. One idea was to kill him with an exploding seashell. Another was to contaminate a wet suit with a fungus that would create a deadly skin infection. The breathing apparatus of the suit

26

THE PLANS TO KILL CASTRO BECAME DECIDEDLY BIZARRE

left *Fidel Castro; CIA attempts on his life, organized under the codename Operation Mongoose, began to resemble something from Mad magazine.*

would also be impregnated with tubercle bacilli for a double threat. The idea was that the suit should be presented to Castro by an unknowing James Donovan, the lawyer who was negotiating the release of the Bay of Pigs prisoners on behalf of Robert Kennedy. This weird scheme might actually have succeeded had not Donovan already made Castro a present of another, perfectly harmless, set of scuba gear.

Other devices conceived to whack the Beard included everything from a machine gun hidden in a TV camera to the inevitable exploding or poisoned cigars. At the time of the Inspector General's report, one deadly cigar from a box intended for Castro, that again used the botulinus toxin, still survived in a CIA storehouse. The cigar was tested and was found not only to have retained 94% of its effectiveness, but was so heavily contaminated with the bacteria that the victim wouldn't even have had to smoke the thing. Simply putting it in his mouth would have been more than enough to kill him.

international community or even a sizeable section of the US people. If an invasion of Cuba was to take place, it would have to be carried out by some kind of proxy force. The invasion might have American support and finance, and be armed with American weapons, but, at least on the surface, it would need to appear to be some kind of popular action by opponents of Castro and his henchmen.

The obvious area for recruitment for this ad hoc army of invasion was among the thousands of Cuban émigrés and refugees who had gathered in Miami and other parts of South Florida since the Castro takeover. Many of these had been members of either Batista's police or armed forces, while others had worked for the US crime bosses like Carlos Marcello and Meyer Lansky. Neither group was a stranger to mayhem and skullduggery. A third potential area of recruitment was among macho young Cubans with no previous military experience, but gung ho and eager to free their homeland from what they saw as the Red Menace. Raising a force was plainly no problem, even though it might be something of a mixed bag. Exactly how it was to be used was another matter.

Even as the anti-Castro forces were being recruited and special CIA training camps established in the Florida Everglades and the jungles of Guatemala, Dulles, Bissell, and their advisors at Langley were still firmly convinced that it only required a sufficiently flamboyant show of force and the majority of the Cuban people would overthrow the Fidelistas and their leftist supporters. A softening-up process began. Saboteurs were dropped into the Cuban countryside to destroy sugar refineries and torch the cane fields. One particularly daring group even set fire to El Encanto, Havana's most prestigious department store. U2 spyplanes maintained a constant surveillance. Small teams of anti-Castro guerrillas were dropped into the mountains of the Sierra Maestra in almost a carbon copy of the way that Fidel himself had started his revolution.

Unfortunately, these opening salvos proved to be way off the mark. Many saboteurs were quickly arrested by armed campesino militia charged with protecting their own vital crops. The guerrillas in the mountains were quickly neutralized by

Castro's troops, many of whom were veterans of the revolution and knew the terrain well. Worst of all, it started to become clear that the Cuban people, far from being disillusioned or hostile to Castro, were prepared to defend their hard-won independence, with their lives if need be.

The Bay of Pigs fiasco

The realization finally began to dawn in the CIA headquarters at Langley that the removal of Fidel Castro wasn't going to be quite as simple as it had first appeared. Richard Bissell immediately revised his plans. The guerrilla warfare trainers were pulled out of the camps in Guatemala and replaced with experts in conventional amphibious assault. New plans called for approximately 1,500 men to effect a D-Day style landing at the beach of Paya Giron on the Bay of Pigs, on the island's southern coast. The landing would be made with full US naval and air support. The force would then push inland and link up with the internal anti-Castro underground that Bissell firmly believed was still widespread in Cuba and only required a sufficiently dashing call to arms to leap into action.

While Bissell was honing and toughening his émigré invasion force, Allen Dulles was experiencing a very different kind of challenge. The invasion of Cuba was being prepared against the background of the 1960 presidential election. The CIA hope was that Eisenhower's Vice President, Richard Nixon, would be installed in the White House, which, certainly on the Cuban front, would pretty much guarantee a continuation of business as usual. Unfortunately for Dulles, and maybe, in the light of subsequent events, for all concerned, this was not to be the case. In November of that year, the American people, by the narrowest of margins, elected John Fitzgerald Kennedy to the office of president.

During the transition period at the end of 1960, Kennedy was briefed in detail by Dulles about the CIA's intentions in Cuba, and gave his tacit approval for a go ahead. The more he studied the Dulles/Bissell plans, however, and consulted with his brother Bobby and other civilian advisors, the more flaws he started to detect. To Kennedy, the invasion seemed far too dependent on active US air and naval support

GUNG HO AND EAGER TO FREE THEIR LAND FROM THE RED MENACE

ever to be able to sell it to the rest of the world as a kind of popular, anti-communist uprising, as had been done with Guatemala. In addition, should the invasion fail, the Bay of Pigs itself was such a dangerously exposed location that any evacuation would put US ships, troops, and aircraft in the very thick of a Dunkirk-style withdrawal. In a memo to Dulles, Kennedy pulled back, firmly ruling out "any direct US troop involvement, or large scale American air support" once the invasion was underway.

Although Dulles assured Kennedy that these limitations would be respected, for all practical purposes he totally ignored the White House directive. He assumed that, if things did go wrong on the beaches at the Bay of Pigs, the new young President would be unable, in the heat of battle, to refuse any needed support.

On April 15th, 1961, CIA-piloted bombers, in a night attack, virtually destroyed Cuba's minuscule air force. Although Nikita Khrushchev had promised Castro Russian-

built MIG fighters, they had not yet been delivered. Two days later, just after midnight, the invasion force hit the beach, only to run head-on into Castro's tanks. Richard Bissell may not have been aware of it, but his invasion force was such a ragtag, and in some cases, dubious bunch—the majority being leftover supporters of the unbelievably corrupt Batista regime—that the plans for the invasion had been leaking like a sieve and Havana was more than ready for them. Instead of pushing quickly inland, the invaders were forced to dig in on the exposed beach and hope that US ships and planes would arrive to pull them out in the nick of time.

It was then that Dulles played what he believed was his trump card. Calling Kennedy in the early hours of the morning, he demanded that the President authorize the ships and planes to bale out the now failing invasion. A furious Kennedy, realizing that he was being openly blackmailed, flatly refused. Apart from some minimal air

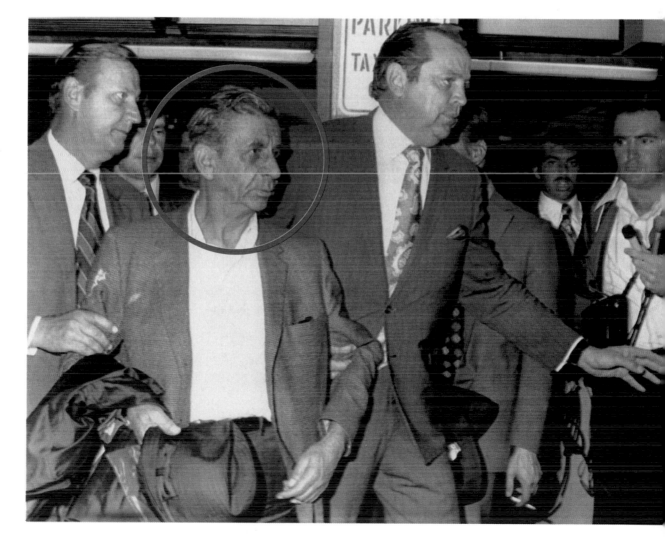

right *Mob boss Meyer Lansky is arrested by Federal agents at Miami Airport. In happier times, Lansky would assist the CIA in their campaign to unseat Castro as payback for Castro closing his Havana casinos*

right *A tank abandoned by the CIA-backed invasion force after their defeat by the Cuban Army at the Bay of Pigs.*

★
30
=

LN 412719   US   LONDON BUREAU
CUBAN INVASION – FIRST PICTURES
HAVANA : ONE OF THE FIRST PICTURES TO BE RECEIVED
BY RADIO FROM HAVANA SINCE THE BEGINNING OF THE
INVASION, APRIL 17TH – IT SHOWS A TANK WITH ITS TREAD
SHOT OFF AT GIRON BEACH, CUBA. CUBANS SAY IT IS
A UNITED STATES TANK.
                          21ST APRIL 1961 PM-HB

UNITED PRESS INTERNATIONAL

cover, the CIA's Cubans were left to extricate themselves from the mess as best they could. According to some theorists, it was in that moment that John F. Kennedy sealed for himself the fate that was to befall him at Dealey Plaza in Dallas.

Although Kennedy went on TV and accepted personal responsibility for the Bay of Pigs fiasco, he privately fumed, declaring at a private dinner party that he was going to "tear down the Agency brick by brick if need be." He felt that he had been set up and then betrayed by his own intelligence network, and he was determined that such a thing would never happen again.

At the other extreme, the CIA firmly believed that Kennedy was making them the fall guys. After Dulles was replaced, former CIA Director James Angleton privately railed against Kennedy: "The Bay of Pigs fiasco was all his doing. I think the decision to withdraw air support colored Kennedy's entire career and impacted on everything that was to follow."

Kennedy moves closer to Cuba

The escalating tension with Cuba would continue until the 1962 October Missile Crisis, but in the breathing space that was created after Kennedy and Khrushchev both stepped back from the brink of nuclear holocaust—to the relief of an entire planet—Kennedy began to rethink seriously his whole attitude to Castro's Cuba. Perhaps confrontation was not the answer. Although he didn't act immediately, through the early part of 1963 he began putting out feelers as to how relations with the Cubans could eventually be normalized. Recently released documents from reports by the Inspector General reveal how Kennedy was cautiously making moves to some sort of rapport with Castro. The first move would be to persuade Castro to free the prisoners captured at the Bay of Pigs. That job fell to Robert Kennedy in his role as Attorney General who, in turn, delegated it to a respected New York lawyer, James Donovan.

above *The White House; prior to JFK's murder, attempts were made toward normalizing relations with Cuba.*

left *John F. Kennedy; although he publicly took the blame for the Bay of Pigs, he vowed to dismantle the CIA as soon as he could. Needless to say, he didn't live that long.*

★
31
=

In October 1963, JFK ordered the CIA to cease all assassination attempts against Castro. He followed this, working through William Atwood, the Special Advisor to the US Delegation at the UN, and bypassing the CIA entirely, by opening low-key negotiations with Carlos Lechuga, the Cuban UN Ambassador. Once again, the CIA decided to ignore the President's orders, and a fresh attempt to kill Castro was instigated by agent Desmond Fitzgerald, although this one, like all of the others, ultimately failed. Even with the CIA attempting to stall progress as much as possible, on November 17th, 1963, Atwood reported that he had been invited to meet with Lechuga in Havana. Suddenly it seemed as though a whole new era was opening up in US-Cuban relations. Then, five days later, Kennedy was dead, shot through the head during his motorcade through Dallas. With Kennedy gone, the idea of a rapprochement with Castro quietly melted away and the Company went back to its more usual routine of propaganda and sabotage.

BY ANY CRITERIA, THE COLD WAR WAS NOT GOING WELL

The period between the Bay of Pigs and the Kennedy assassination was a nadir for the CIA. Even its supposed successes, like the removal of Patrice Lumumba, the Congolese Leader who, in their opinion was getting too chummy with the Russians and Chinese, and Ngo Dinh Diem, the Vietnamese premier who was starting to prove a thorn in the side of early US efforts in Vietnam, couldn't entirely wipe out the memory of the Cuban debacle. Kennedy's successor, Lyndon Johnson, may have had no desire to "tear down the agency brick by brick," but he was hardly enthusiastic about the role that they had played up to this point. By any criteria, the Cold War was not going well. In Indochina, the French had been forced to concede the northern part of their former colony to the communists under Ho Chi Minh. Castro was firmly entrenched in Cuba, and, apart from the abortive 1956 uprising in Hungary, the Soviets retained a solid lock on Eastern Europe. If all this wasn't bad enough,

the Russians now had missiles able to bring down CIA U2 spyplanes. Meanwhile, at home, individuals like journalist Mark Lane and New Orleans District Attorney Jim Garrison were beginning to ask, in the wake of the highly unsatisfactory Warren Commission, if the CIA had played any role in the assassination of JFK, and were demanding to know what the Agency's connections might be to the supposed "lone gunman," Lee Harvey Oswald.

The Company needed damage control, and what better way to start than to postulate a global threat against which they would be America's foremost bulwark. The notorious Domino Theory began to gain popularity, the basis of which was that all the evil in the world could be attributed to the menace of international communism. The tunnel vision of the 1950s degenerated into a state of total myopia. Within the CIA, the idea wasn't even entertained that revolutionary movements around the world might be primarily concerned with getting out from under former colonial rule and asserting their own national identity, or even with the fundamental motive of seeking a better standard of living for their people.

In the early 1960s, the Company saw nothing but the Red Conspiracy. Military historian Harry Summers observed: "We bought the communist myth. The peculiarly

left *The Viet Cong triggered US fears of the downfall of democratic governments all across Asia and gave rise to the notorious domino theory.*

American fallacy." This was a fallacy that every supposed communist threat was merely a tentacle that could eventually be traced back to the head of this giant octopus in Moscow and the Kremlin; by 1964, Vietnam had replaced Cuba as the most threatening tentacle. Lyndon Johnson, privately over drinks with friends, summed up the Domino Theory and the seemingly crucial position of Vietnam in his typically down home terms: "Give up Vietnam and you wind up losing India. That's the plain truth. They're out to get us, and don't think they're not! If you let a bully pick on your helpless neighbor today, why, tomorrow he'll kick you out of your front yard. And if you let him do that, the next day he'll kick you out of your living room. And ..." Johnson had suddenly stiffened and glared around at the circle of listeners, "... the day after that, he'll be upstairs raping your wife in your own bed." In this and similar, if less flamboyant, statements, Johnson not only reconfirmed the Company's long-held world view but also defined the next crucial trouble spot. It was clear that CIA involvement in Vietnam could provide both the perfect opportunity for the Agency to restore its tarnished prestige, and the chance to test all of its hardware and know-how in a full-scale war, without the kind of limitations it felt had been its downfall in Cuba. The Company decided that, as far as possible, Vietnam was going to be its very own war.

The Phoenix Program

The centerpiece of all CIA efforts during the course of the war had to be the notorious "Phoenix Program." The Phoenix Program, under the leadership of William Colby,

recognized that Vietnam was a war being conducted on two very different fronts. On one hand, the North Vietnamese Army was waging a fairly conventional war in the North. On the other, the Viet Cong were fighting a highly sophisticated guerrilla war, both in the countryside and even in the heart of South Vietnam's major cities. The regular US Army, Air Force, and Marines were figured to be more than capable of handling the conventional war. The CIA would devote the majority of their energies and resources to combating the Viet Cong.

From the very start, Colby made the same fundamental mistake that so many of his CIA predecessors had made. He took the elitist position that an army, seemingly poorly armed, and dressed in what looked like black pajamas, could hardly prevail against a superpower like the USA. It seemed to have failed to occur to anyone at Langley that the VC might conceivably be the best guerrilla fighters in the world. For almost a thousand years, the Vietnamese had been fighting off foreign invaders. Only a decade earlier they had routed the French, and they had guerrilla tactics down to such a fine art, it seemed that they could strike, vanish, and then reappear again at will.

This is not, however, to underestimate the energy that Colby and his men put into their war in Vietnam. Centered in Saigon, and cloaking everything in the banner of national security, the first phase of Operation Phoenix was, as far

TURN SOUTH VIETNAM INTO A POLITICAL POLICE STATE

left The AK47 assault rifle, widely used by communist troops and guerrillas. Simply constructed, it could be repaired by the village blacksmith.

above The American .30-calibre machine gun. US weaponry was plagued by technical problems.

as possible, to turn South Vietnam into a political police state of Orwellian proportions. A vast network of spies and informers was constructed, from the village level all the way to the corridors of power. For the first time, computers were used in a counter-terrorism operation. Vast blacklists were compiled of suspected VC and VC sympathizers. When the list for a certain area seemed more or less comprehensive, hunter-killer teams of assassins would be sent out to eliminate as many on the list as they could locate. No evidence was produced, no trial was conducted. Under the auspices of Phoenix, suspicion was as good as guilt, and guilt invariably meant a summary death sentence, possibly preceded by a period of interrogation and torture.

The conflict between the CIA and Viet Cong had to be one of the strangest matchings of contenders since Custer and the 7th Cavalry fought Sitting Bull and the Sioux. On one hand, the CIA had access to hundreds of millions of dollars, hardware ranging from the B52 bomber to state-of-the-art computers and the ComSat satellite system. On the

other hand, the average Viet Cong lived on a bowl of rice a day if need be, and was armed with an AK47 sub-machine-gun if he was lucky. However, he could tunnel like a strategic mole, while intelligence gathering female VC agents would enlist as strippers and hookers in the bars and brothels frequented by US combat troops on R&R (rest and relaxation) furloughs. The Viet Cong resorted to such low-tech measures as catapulting tinfoil balls into the air from between two trees to confuse the radar of US fighter jets. In terms of science fiction—and much of the Vietnam war had a strange habit of starting to look like science fiction—it seemed to be a conflict of the organic against the machine.

The PSYOPS campaign

Hard as the Viet Cong might have been, though, the CIA machine's combination of terror and reward—Phoenix operatives would pay as much as $20,000 for a crucial name or piece of information—proved highly effective. As far as can be ascertained from what records have been made public over the years, at least 20,000 suspects died as a result of the Phoenix Program, and some estimates put the number twice as high as that. Assassination, however, was only one of the wings of the Phoenix. Money and manpower was also poured into a huge campaign of psychological warfare, tactics that would be known ever after as PSYOPS. Historian Douglas Valentine describes how Phoenix brought its PSYOP campaign into play: "Because fear of the Phoenix Program was an effective means of creating informers and defectors, an intensive publicity campaign called 'the Popular Information Program' was instituted. Psywar teams crisscrossed the country using Phoenix-supplied radios, leaflets, posters, TV shows, movies, banners, and loudspeakers mounted on sampans to get the message across." The message was a simple one—"root out the evil commies in your midst."

In many respects, the CIA were not only fighting in Vietnam for the obvious objective of defeating the Viet Cong; Vietnam provided the perfect test bed for weapons that had waited in readiness through most of the Cold War. Everything from the B52 bomber to defoliants like Agent Orange could be put through their paces under full combat conditions. In the case of the CIA's PSYOP techniques, Vietnam was the culmination of experimental programs by ultra-secret research sections like MKULTRA, going all the way back to the OSS and the material that they had brought out of Dachau and the other caches of Nazi data.

Vietnam was also the time and place that the CIA started to believe that perhaps all things really were

above *"Me love you longtime, Joe." Many South Vietnam bar girls and prostitutes were, in fact, VC agents.*

★
35
=

OPERATION WANDERING SOUL

Possibly the most bizarre of the Phoenix Program PSYOP was the one that went by the codename "Operation Wandering Soul." Light aircraft were equipped with powerful loudspeakers and flew high over remote rural villages broadcasting prerecorded tapes in Vietnamese that purported to be the voices of the inhabitants' ancestors. The "ancestors" advised their descendants below to have no dealings with the communists, and immediately to report any who might approach them to the authorities. The thinking behind this strange and spooky scheme was that the average Vietnamese peasant was so backward that he would unhesitatingly follow the instructions of their great-great-grandparents. At the same time, the VC were conducting literacy and political education classes in their villages!

possible. Saigon rapidly became a never-never land of strange alliances and secret treaties. Although Operation Phoenix was both devious and deadly, it had a certain straightforward sense of mission. Its objectives were clear and, although the methods might have been loathsome, they at least went directly to their designated target.

Air America

When the Company moved into more peripheral areas, things became a lot less defined. A perfect example is that of the supposedly commercial airline, Air America. Air America, although wholly owned and operated by the CIA, functioned to all outward appearances like an independent, small-time cargo carrier. Obviously, there had to be times when the Agency needed to move men and material with a degree of secrecy that would not have been possible using normal military transport planes. When, however, the operation started to take on a life and purpose of its own, the waters became extremely muddy.

The most famous example of this kind of bizarre free enterprise was, of course, the trade in arms for drugs that

★
36
=

right *Loading an Air America DC3. The CIA used these planes to ferry its own operatives, clandestine equipment and drugs.*

left *Opium poppies and packages of refined heroin. Raw opium became one of Air America's prime cargoes.*

RAW OPIUM FOUND ITS WAY BACK TO SAIGON IN THE FORM OF HEROIN

took place between the CIA and Air America and the various anti-communist guerrilla groups fighting the Pathet Lao—the Laotian equivalent of the Viet Cong—in the neighboring country of Laos. Once again, the Company fell into the trap of requiring no further credentials than that an individual or group was against the communists before doing business with them. In the case of the Laotian anti-communists, many of them were also the country's largest opium producers, and their war with the Pathet Lao was less one of ideology than a simple desire to protect their business interests and their poppy fields from the insurgents. Air America was used extensively to ferry in arms, ammunition, and CIA advisors to the Laotian anti-communists. Unfortunately, Air America found that, in return, it was flying out with the same people's raw opium which, after being refined in Thailand, found its way back to Saigon in the form of heroin, and then went on sale to the US troops in the jungles and rice paddies. As usual, the CIA never seemed to be aware when it was advancing into potential quicksand.

As usual, the Company also found it hard to learn from its mistakes. A similar setup was sponsored by Colonel Oliver North during the Iran-Contra chaos, when Agency-chartered aircraft would fly arms down to the Nicaraguan Contras in their base camps in Honduras, apparently to return with crack cocaine that would eventually wind up being sold on the streets of South Central Los Angeles and elsewhere.

Even though, in the end, the Americans, the CIA included, would be forced out of Vietnam, it was the place where the Company learned many of its most ruthless lessons and developed some of its most chilling techniques. The notorious CIA Interrogation Manual was honed and refined during the era of the Phoenix Program, and indeed, the Phoenix Program itself, once sharpened and codified, would be taught to a variety of right-wing military dictatorships in Latin America at the notorious School of the Americas at Fort Benning, Georgia. The overall war in Vietnam may have proved a military defeat for the United States, but for the CIA, it was also the proving ground for some of its most frightening theories and would set the tone for Company actions in the years to come.

UP, UP, AND AWAY

One hellishly ingenious interrogation technique that CIA director William Colby's operatives employed during the course of the Phoenix Program, and often referred to as the "sky dive" or "taking the fall," involved taking some five or six suspected Viet Cong or Viet Cong sympathizers up in a helicopter for questioning.

The chopper would rise to an altitude of about 500 feet and then the first suspect would be questioned in a quick and perfunctory manner. If he or she wasn't immediately forthcoming with the required answers, they would simply be thrown out of the open door of the helicopter to fall to their deaths. The same thing would happen to a second, and then a third suspect. The theory was that by the time the remaining one or two prisoners had seen all of their comrades tossed out into space, they would be more than ready to spill whatever beans their interrogators expected of them.

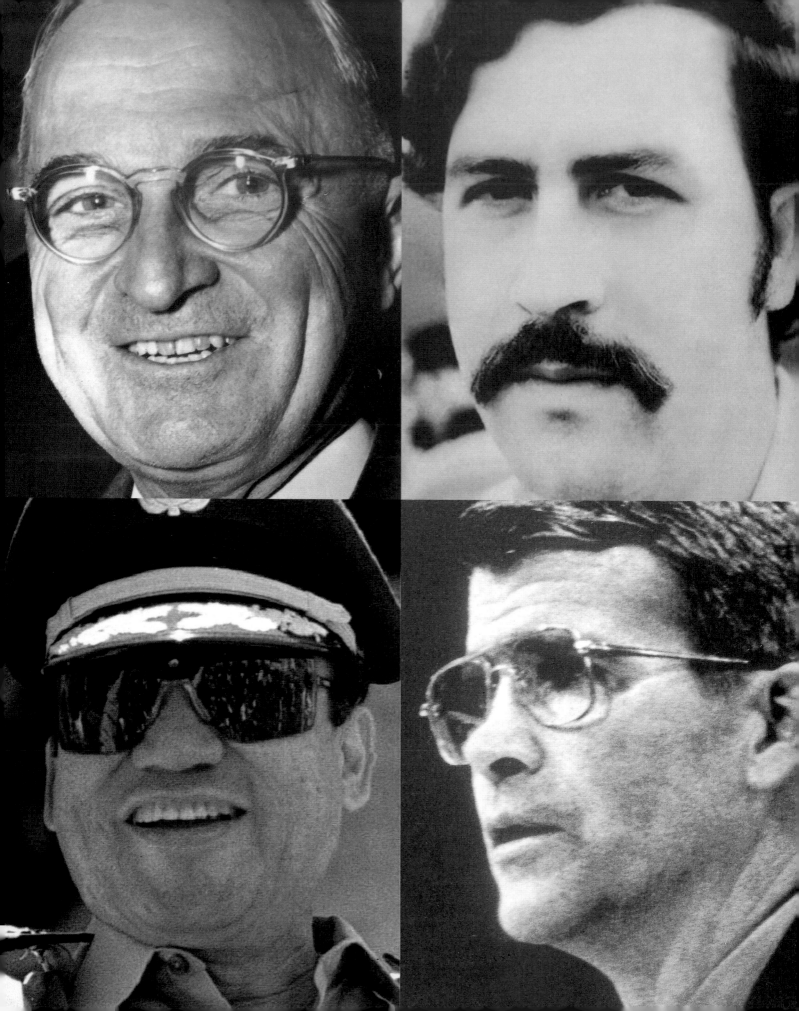

CHAPTER TWO

THE SHADOW GOVERNMENT

Who's in Charge Here?

"If you drop a frog into a pot of boiling water, it will immediately leap out, trying to save its life. If, on the other hand, you place the same frog in a pot of lukewarm water, it will happily remain there. Slowly bring the water to the boil and the frog will not move. It will sit there until it dies."

It is less than clear which political philosopher first used this unpleasant experiment with the unfortunate frog as a metaphor for the slow takeover of a nation or a culture. Some attribute it to Machiavelli, others to either V.I.Lenin, Heinrich Himmler, J. Edgar Hoover, or even Sun–tzu, author of *The Art Of War*. What's not in doubt is that, over the course of the last half century, it has been regularly applied to the methods and agendas of the Central Intelligence Agency.

The founding of the CIA

Although initially the 1947 National Security Act that created the CIA was a pretty tightly designed document in terms of preventing the Agency from becoming any kind of state police—the specific fear was of creating an American Gestapo—it was almost immediately provided with a number of

facing page *Who's in charge here? (clockwise from top left) President Harry S. Truman, who approved the setting up of the CIA; Colombian drug lord, Pablo Escobar; Colonel Oliver North, who ran wars from the basement of the Reagan White House; Panama's ex-strongman, Manuel Noriega.*

right *CIA Headquarters, Langley, Virginia—the Fortress of Freedom or the Heart of Darkness?*

loopholes that gave the Agency and its director a great deal more freedom of movement than was ever originally intended. A directive titled NSC-4 began to heat the proverbial pot by empowering "the Secretary of State to coordinate overseas information activities designed to counter communism." An addendum, NSC-4A, also gave the CIA the power to "undertake covert actions." In these three words, the Agency was transformed from the data coordination operation that had been initially envisioned to an aggressive pro-active clandestine warfare center, one that would eventually see itself as something very close to an alternative government for the United States and a power in the world that, quite literally, respected no boundaries or frontiers.

Two later directives—NSC-10/1 and NSC-10/2, that expanded covert activities and even validated certain "extralegal practices"—gave the CIA more espionage elbow room than they could ever have reasonably hoped for. The purpose of these directives was to provide a buffer between the Agency and the president that would allow the president to deny all knowledge if any problematic CIA actions accidentally became public. They also permitted the CIA to keep secrets from the president himself. As the years passed, NSC-10/1 and NSC-10/2 would serve—as in the case of the Bay of Pigs and other covert CIA adventures—to keep the president in the dark as to the Agency's purpose or practical agendas, making the director of the CIA the near-absolute king of his own, very mysterious hill, and giving him virtual carte blanche for his agency to do whatever it liked as long as it fell into the general category of "countering communism."

When, in 1953, Allen Dulles became CIA director, this elbow room was quietly eased à point closer to total autonomy. The CIA was then effectively responsible to no one and could, in theory, become a law totally unto itself—a de facto shadow government—able to make and implement policy under a cloak of "need to know" secrecy that could exclude absolutely anyone from the loop of information. Back with our unhappy frog, the water was coming to the boil and it didn't know a damn thing about it.

Winston Churchill once remarked, regarding espionage and counter-espionage, that "truth is so precious that she must be surrounded by a bodyguard of lies." The CIA seemed to take that maxim a stage further—truth was so precious, it couldn't be entrusted to the American public. Predating Jack Nicholson's famous line in the movie *A Few Good Men* by nearly half a century, the CIA started to act as though the American people "weren't ready for the truth, they couldn't handle the truth." This was ironic in the extreme for an organization that has the motto "And ye shall know the truth and the truth shall make you free" inscribed in marble on the wall of the main entrance lobby in its headquarters.

Having quickly maneuvered itself into a position where the only controls over its conduct came from within, one of the CIA's first actions plainly indicated that restraint, especially moral restraint, had a very low priority inside the Company. It quickly started playing a major role in the electoral process in many of the European democracies that were emerging from the devastation of World War Two. Using money, propaganda, and influence, the Company became a major player in seeing that the communists were

TRUTH WAS SO PRECIOUS, IT COULDN'T BE ENTRUSTED TO THE PUBLIC

defeated in the 1948 Italian elections, and that the Labor Party won a major victory in Israel. Similar moves were also made in the elections of neighboring Latin American countries like Mexico and Colombia. The process of election manipulation reached such a level that Miles Copeland, an early CIA power broker (and the father of Stewart Copeland, drummer in The Police) described it thus: "In an election in such-and-such a country, the KGB backs a candidate, the CIA backs a candidate, and the CIA candidate wins."

The CIA also seems to have decided that what was good for foreigners might also be good for the USA. Certainly, as early as 1952 the US Presidential elections were crucial to the Agency's very survival. The CIA was not only under fire from Democrats in both Congress and the White House,

★
41
=

THE STRANGE DEATH OF A SECRETARY OF DEFENSE

Rumors have circulated for the last 50 years that, even immediately after its creation, the CIA was quite prepared to kill anyone that it saw as threatening its survival, and that one of the first victims of this killer arrogance was none other than a US Secretary of Defense. In the wake of War World Two, James Forrestal—then Secretary of the Navy in the Truman administration—had been an enthusiastic supporter of the idea that the country should have a centralized intelligence operation. When he subsequently became Secretary of Defense, he started to object to the obsessive secrecy that was developing in the new agency. He opposed the provisions NSC-10/1 and NSC-10/2 and lobbied for the Agency to be brought under much tighter government control, and that would appear to have been James Forrestal's downfall.

In his admittedly contentious book, Behold A Pale Horse, ex-Naval Intelligence Officer William Cooper recounts Forrestal's alleged fate: "Rightfully, he believed he was being watched. This was interpreted by those who were ignorant of the facts as paranoia. Forrestal later was said to have suffered a nervous breakdown. He was ordered to the mental ward of Bethesda Naval Hospital....He had to be isolated and discredited. His family and friends were denied permission to visit. Finally, on May 21, 1949, Forrestal's brother made a fateful decision. He notified the authorities that he intended to remove James from Bethesda on May 22. Some time in the early morning of May 22, 1949, agents of the CIA tied a sheet around James Forrestal's neck, fastened the other end to a fixture in his room, then threw [him] out of the window. The sheet tore and he plummeted to his death. The CIA confiscated his secret diaries."

still being seen as a potential "American Gestapo," but FBI Director J. Edgar Hoover was also doing all he could to shut down the fledgling rival. The Company desperately needed a victory by the Republican candidate and staunch CIA supporter, General Dwight D. Eisenhower, to keep itself in business. In 1952, the Agency hardly had the clout to influence a national election significantly but, from that point on, it did what it could for the candidate of its choice. By the election of 1972, it had become such a skilled and powerful political player that it was supplying agents and ex-agents to run Richard Nixon's "dirty tricks" operation, the one which would ultimately self-destruct in the Watergate scandal.

When Eisenhower was elected, Allen Dulles took over the CIA and his brother John ran the State Department; the CIA had not only survived, but now went far beyond the mere manipulation of the electoral process. It began to move into the business of the actual removal of foreign governments—ones that it either didn't like or were considered bad for American corporate interests. The first of these political amputations took place in Iran and, on many levels, the world has been paying the price ever since.

Influence abroad: Teheran, 1953

In 1953, rioting in the streets of Teheran, the capital of Iran, ended the democratic, socialist-leaning government of Prime Minister Mohammed Mosaddeq, and the Shah was returned to power. These outbreaks of government-toppling rioting had been bought and paid for by a small CIA secret task force headed by Kermit Roosevelt, the grandson of President Theodore Roosevelt. Armed with nothing more lethal than a million dollars in cash, they had brought down "the pinko Mosaddeq," and the Company was pretty damned pleased with itself.

To their way of thinking, they had headed off Mosaddeq's stated intention of nationalizing "colonialist" oil installations and had made Iran safe for Gulf, Standard Oil, Mobil, and Texaco, and also the British oil giant BP. Roosevelt and what he referred to as his "cowboys" also believed that they had prevented the formation of a possible Moslem, pro-Soviet power bloc in the Middle East and had maybe saved the state of Israel into the bargain. What they didn't realize was that they had created a whirlwind that would be reaped at the end of the 1970s with the US embassy's Iran hostage crisis and that would be the driving force behind a dangerously angry Moslem fundamentalism that poses a threat to US security today –

left CIA-orchestrated rioting in Iran brings down the government of Prime Minister Mohammed Mosaddeq (inset) and puts the Shah back in power.

and that looks as though it will continue to do so well into the twenty-first century.

The CIA, however, didn't seem too interested in long-term projections back then. It had discovered that it had the capability of rearranging other countries and changing and replacing their governments like so many pieces on a game board. Like a kid with a new toy, it was looking around for other candidates on which to flex its new-found covert muscles. After Iran, it was the turn of Guatemala, and then the Dominican Republic. Cuba may have presented more of a problem, as did Vietnam, but the remainder of the list of CIA-instigated coups and revolutions reads like a compliant atlas—the people of Bolivia, the Philippines, El Salvador, Nicaragua, Chile, Argentina, Jamaica, Burma, the Congo, and at least a half dozen more sovereign nations all had the dubious pleasure of having the CIA attempt to control who ruled them. Some of those on the list can be dismissed as either Third World emergent nations or banana republics with little experience of how to govern themselves, but others were powerful long-term allies.

Rumors circulated at the time that the CIA had tried and failed to prevent the election of Harold Wilson in Britain in 1966. Indira Gandhi complained to the United Nations that the Company was using money, manpower, and dirty tricks to undermine her ruling Indian Congress Party. Possibly most amazing of all, the available evidence suggests that the Agency, in 1975, brought down the Australian Labor government of Prime Minister E. Gough Whitlam. Apparently, the CIA was bitter that Whitlam had,

three years earlier, pulled his country out of the Vietnam War, and also feared that he would withdraw Australian consent for the CIA to operate its vast, ultra-secret, southern hemisphere communications center at Pine Gap in the Australian outback.

This interference with the governments of supposedly friendly countries might have been to some degree excused had the American Central Intelligence Agency at least been attempting to spread an American-style constitutional democracy. All too often, however, a left-of-center, popular or maybe nationalist democracy would be replaced by a brutally repressive, fascist, or military dictatorship. The reasons for overthrowing governments and funding coups and uprisings often became hard to reconcile with the avowed US aims of freedom, liberty, and justice for all. Many covert operations would seem merely to be staged to oblige the most crass US business interests. Others seemed to emanate from nothing more than the bizarre world view of the men who controlled the Agency. In the war against communism, the CIA not only espoused the theory that the enemies of one's enemies had, by definition, to be one's friends, but took it to such absurd extremes that the question began to be asked if the Company was running

a foreign policy all of its own, with little or nothing in common with the avowed intentions of the people or government of the United States.

Stansfield Turner: an attempt at morality

It wasn't until Jimmy Carter appointed Admiral Stansfield Turner, a respected NATO commander—and a comparative outsider—as Director of the CIA in 1977 that the reservations were finally voiced. "There are rules that this country wants followed" he said, and Turner was going make damned sure that the Agency followed them, at least on his watch. He and Carter—both former naval officers—wanted their intelligence operatives to concentrate on high-tech information gathering and phase out the dirty tricks, international manipulations, destabilizations, and quasi-military covert ops. Unfortunately Turner's watch wouldn't outlast the Carter administration. When Ronald Reagan came to power, one of his first moves was make William Casey, a "good old boy" veteran of the OSS, the

head of the Agency, and things settled back to the mindset that was petulantly summed up by Richard Helms in a TV interview: "Why do we have to take our ideas overseas?" As far as Casey and Helms were concerned, the rules certainly didn't apply outside of the USA. The Agency seemed willing to support any one who claimed to be an anti-communist no matter how monstrous and repressive their own politics, and consideration had to be given to the suspicion that the CIA was, in fact, spreading a new kind of fascism of its own devising. Indeed, that it really was acting as the shadow government of the USA and—maybe in its ultimate dreams—of the whole world. It may have been set up as the eyes and ears of the US government, but it had also decided that it should be the controlling brain.

In the 1950s and 1960s, and to a lesser degree in the Reagan 1980s, these doubts were expressed and questions asked, but they were asked very quietly. If the CIA bothered to answer at all, its response was simple: they were the

THE RULES CERTAINLY DIDN'T APPLY OUTSIDE OF THE USA

right *President Jimmy Carter wanted the CIA to concentrate on high-tech intelligence gathering and phase out the dirty tricks and covert operations*

CIA, they had the real goods in terms of intelligence and information, and they alone knew what was best. If they wanted to support Pinochet in Chile, the military junta in Argentina, or Papa Doc Duvalier in Haiti, it was in the best interests of the USA, and anyone who questioned their view was either a fool, a communist, or a traitor and deserved, at the very least, to be on some kind of list.

More than anything else, this elitist attitude that "the Company knows best" generated the concern that all too often the CIA was not truly operating in the best interests of the USA at all, but according to some murky agenda know only to the Agency itself. The upper echelons of the Company might feel that the two things were one and the same but, over the years, as stories of their more dubious adventures began emerge into the light of day, it became harder and harder to argue that this was indeed the case. Could it really be in the broad interests of the American people to form alliances with fascist dictators, conduct experiments in mind control, test chemical and bacterial covert warfare on unsuspecting citizens, and make deals with gangsters and drug dealers? The idea took root that

maybe the CIA, with its iron-clad cult of secrecy, could ultimately wield more power than either Congress or the president. This fear was particularly pronounced during the Vietnam era when, under the pretext of neutralizing the Viet Cong, the CIA not only seemed to be exploring the very heart of darkness with operations like the brutally ruthless Phoenix Program, but also running an increasing number of domestic offensives directed at individuals and groups opposed to the war.

Moving into FBI territory

The CIA was expressly forbidden from keeping files on US citizens, but it did it anyway, not only ignoring the law, but also risking the wrath of FBI Director Hoover by invading his jealously guarded turf. At first, the Company stayed within its designated boundaries, not so much out of respect for the National Security Act but because the early Agency wasn't strong enough to challenge Hoover on his home ground. Very quickly, though, the lines grew blurred. Espionage is played out on a global chessboard, and it

THE SEARCH FOR NON-EXISTENT KGB AGENTS AT HARVARD

employed or contracted by them. Gradually, a grudging accommodation was hammered out between the Company and the FBI on the matter of domestic operations. Even the notoriously territorial Hoover realized that he had to cut Allen Dulles and his successors at Langley a certain amount of slack to avoid the creation of dangerously embarrassing jurisdictional confusion. This didn't mean, however, that problems of where FBI territory ended and the CIA's began didn't constantly occur.

The real confusion of who was to spy on whom started with the covert war on Fidel Castro. One of the main bases of CIA operations against revolutionary Cuba had, by necessity, to be in the Cuban émigré community in Miami. Anti-Castro guerrillas were being trained in the Everglades, clandestine flights were going out from airstrips all over South Florida, and boatloads of CIA-backed saboteurs were slipping out of the Keys. All of these operations had to be monitored for possible enemy infiltrators and the Company also felt the need to keep tabs on Castro's representatives at the United Nations in New York. Liaison also had to be maintained with mobsters like Carlos Marcello and Meyer Lansky who, with their Havana hotels and casinos, had controlled a major slice of the pre-revolutionary Cuban economy and had contacts vital to the Agency's anti-Castro efforts.

And then President John Kennedy was shot. The fury of rumor, speculation, theory, and paranoia that surrounded the Kennedy assassination very much forced the FBI and the CIA to close ranks. Fingers were being pointed at both agencies. What were the CIA connections with Lee Harvey Oswald, the supposed assassin? Had Oswald been a CIA operative? How was it the FBI didn't know Oswald was in Dallas in November 1963? If any conspiracy existed, both the FBI and the CIA would find themselves uncomfortably close to the center of the action. They figured in a major way in the assassination scenarios being promoted by journalists like Mark Lane and Jack Anderson and by New Orleans District Attorney Jim Garrison during his prosecution of alleged conspirator Clay Shaw. Tarred by the same conspiracist brush, the CIA and FBI were forced to work together—if only to keep the Warren Commission's hasty explanation of the lone gunman in place.

hardly made sense that, if an Agency enemy entered the domestic United States, the CIA should hand the entire case over to the FBI. Even with the best possible inter-agency cooperation, such a situation would create massive loopholes that the bad guys could all too easily exploit.

The CIA also conducted its research and development in the USA itself. For the testing of spyplanes to the work of groups like MKULTRA, the CIA needed secure areas inside the USA, and the power to protect its installations and conduct background checks on those who might be

right *The CIA's aptly named CHAOS unit infiltrated the Vietnam War protest movement, but failed to find connections with Iron Curtain governments.*

left *Black Panther Leader Eldridge Cleaver in custody. Cleaver was luckier than some of his fellow Panthers who were simply killed by Federal agents.*

COINTELPRO and CHAOS

By this point, however, America was rolling headlong into the strife and conflict of the 1960s. The mindset of both agencies virtually guaranteed that J. Edgar Hoover and Richard Helms would quickly agree that America as they knew it was in the gravest danger, both from within and without. When the CIA proposed its own domestic surveillance and harassment program, Hoover reluctantly went along with it. For the first time, the CIA and FBI began to work together with only a minimum of professional jealously. While the FBI's COINTELPRO spied on radical groups, harassed peace organizations and executed many of the leaders of the Black Panther Party, the CIA's Operation CHAOS opened mail, tapped phones, penetrated anti-war organizations, and set up campus front organizations to pinpoint "dangerous student agitators." The Agency also spread hundreds of agents through anti-war groups in other countries, with particular emphasis on Britain, France, Germany, Sweden, and Canada.

Later it would be plain even to Director Helms that the student radical-peace movement-black power-hippie coalition was a spontaneous and self-generating movement, and not controlled from Moscow, Peking, Havana, or Hanoi,

but it took the CIA a very long time to come to this realization. Massive amounts of money and energy were wasted on the search for non-existent KGB agents at Harvard or in Haight Ashbury. It was almost as though the Agency, having fermented insurrection and discontent in so many other countries, couldn't believe that the same wasn't being done by an enemy power inside the US. As late as 1967, according to author Rhodri Jeffreys-Jones, both Helms and Lyndon Johnson firmly believed that "the domestic protest movement against the Vietnam War was being externally orchestrated" and expected CHAOS and COINTELPRO to put a stop to it.

Even though, by the mid-1960s, the CIA and the FBI might have finally been working somewhat in tandem, the Company's domestic ops were still totally illegal. Like "Wild Bill" Donovan during World War Two, Helms and his cohorts had obviously decided that, in time of war, legality no longer mattered. Unfortunately, the CIA was, in part, fighting a war against its own people, and the belief grew that the CIA was slowly but steadily reaching for unacceptable levels of power. This idea flourished not least among the hundreds of thousands of American citizens who had their lives invaded by CIA agents for no other reason than that they disagreed with the war in South East Asia.

The secrets of Mount Weather

More detailed rumors spread about an ultra-secret facility at Mount Weather, near the small town of Bluemont, Virginia. Built in the early 1950s as part of a nuclear preparedness civil defense program, and designed to act as an alternative seat of government in the event of an atomic attack, Mount Weather was reputed to be a virtual underground city. It was also alleged to be the repository for all the data gathered on US citizens by CHAOS and similar CIA domestic ops. In 1975, John Tunney, chairman of the Subcommittee on Constitution Rights, charged that over 100,000 detailed and highly illegal dossiers on USA citizens were stored on the Mount Weather computers, and that a list of some 15,000 names were maintained of individuals who would be immediately detained in a situation of national emergency. When

THEY KEEP US IN THE DARK AND FEED US A LOT OF MANURE

Tunney's committee questioned General Leslie Bray, director of the Federal Preparedness Agency about Mount Weather, its function, and its use by the FBI and CIA, they ran into a stone wall. Bray's reply was brief and uncooperative. "I am not at liberty to describe precisely what is the role and the mission and the capability we have at Mount Weather." As far as anyone knows, it is still there and still in operation. Information is still being gathered and none of its dossiers have ever been deleted.

The basis of most of the accusations that the CIA is—or at least has designs on being—a secret government, are based on a simple litmus test. Does the Company control the government or does the government control the Company? Clearly the CIA has never paid too much heed to either the demands or intentions of the legislative body. Lying to congressional

★
48
=

SPYCAT

Even while the CIA was making itself one of the most feared and distrusted organizations in the world, it was, on occasion, simultaneously able to sink to levels of witlessness more worthy of the Three Stooges. A perfect example was the case of the spycat radio transmitter. The absurd incident was reported in Victor Marchetti's book *The CIA and the Cult Of Intelligence*, but was later censored with the agreement of the publishers. One of the CIA technical research outfits was seemingly grappling with the problem that it was very hard to eavesdrop at Washington cocktail parties with just a static microphone. The background noise was too distracting and people on whom listening agents wanted to focus tended to move around and socialize too much. Something had to be done. The various parties at the Washington embassies were considered fertile ground by the Agency, the ideal location for loose talk and drunken indiscretions.

The plan was devised to surgically implant a miniature transmitter in the body cavity of an ordinary domestic cat, with an antenna running beneath the skin of the unfortunate animal's tail. The cat was expected to circulate freely at the party and pick up a broad cross section of the conversation. The microphone that fed signals to the transmitter was implanted in the cat's ear, the theory being that the cat would move its ears, "focusing" on particular conversations in much the same way that a human would. According to Marchetti, the project had cost more than a million dollars of taxpayers' money before it was supposedly perfected.

Finally, the "spycat" was ready for testing and let loose at a trial party. The CIA scientists and agents—headphones clamped in place, tape recorders running—waited tensely at a nearby listening station to discover how their feline brainchild would perform in the field. They quickly discovered, to their dismay, that the animal had an agenda of its own. After being shooed away from the canapés, the cat found something that interested it much more than any diplomatic indiscretion. A noise behind the baseboard indicated the presence of a mouse, and the cat spent the remainder of the party investigating. Seemingly not even a multi-million dollar budget could make a cat interested in espionage when a mouse was around!

above *Harry S. Truman, who set the CIA in motion and rubber stamped their early operations.*

right *Ex-CIA Watergate conspirators G. Gordon Liddy and E. Howard Hunt, and (below) their boss Richard Nixon. The names of Hunt and Liddy constantly recur in the history of CIA covert ops and dirty tricks.*

oversight committees has become both a fine art and standard practice for CIA directors during the life of the Company, to the point that in 1982—as Ronald Reagan was giving the agency a virtual free hand under William Casey—Representative Norman Mineta of the House Intelligence Committee, bitterly remarked: "We are like mushrooms. They keep us in the dark and feed us a lot of manure." From the National Security Act that created the agency to the Boland Amendment in the 1980s, which prohibited the CIA from aiding the Nicaraguan Contras, the US Congress has passed laws to limit the powers of the CIA, and the Agency, in its turn, has ignored, sidestepped or circumvented them.

If Congress is unable effectively to reign in the CIA, it must logically follow that the crucial relationship is the one between the Company and the President of the United States. Which one is really in the driver's seat? Through its half century of life, the CIA has dealt with ten presidents. Truman was wary, while Eisenhower pretty much rubber stamped anything it did. Kennedy vowed to close it down, but didn't live long enough to make good his promise. Lyndon Johnson, especially in the prosecution of the war in Vietnam, went along with just about everything the Agency did, no matter how excessive. Richard Nixon saw the Company as his personal goon squad and even used ex-operatives like E. Howard Hunt and G. Gordon Liddy to run

below *When Ronald Reagan took over the White House, the CIA went back to business as usual.*

★
50
=

THE NEW WORLD ORDER

dirty tricks and extra-legal activities for his 1972 reelection campaign. After Watergate and Nixon's resignation, the CIA found itself in as much disarray as the country itself. All Gerald Ford could do was maintain a holding operation. Jimmy Carter, on the other hand—a one-time nuclear submarine commander who had little patience with the wilder antics of the Agency—brought in Stansfield Turner to reform the CIA, only to find himself deceived, undermined, and, as far as possible, shut out of the loop. Suspicions even linger that the CIA may have had a hand in Carter's defeat by Ronald Reagan in the 1980 presidential election.

Ronald Reagan voluntarily took the process of isolating the president one major step further. He wasn't cut out of the loop, he wanted out. At least, this is what his actions would seem to indicate. All through his two term presidency, the Great Communicator opted for the bland smile, a hand cupped to the deaf ear, and unlimited plausible deniability. "What did the president know and when did he know it?" became the key question in

The suspicion that the world might be controlled by some highly secret group of the ultra-elite dates back to the time when humanity first started to think about itself in global terms. Secret societies and nomadic minorities, religious sects and mystic Tibetans, space aliens and computers with artificial intelligence, have all been accused at various times of "really running the planet." One of the most recent group of these mystery rulers is the New World Order. The idea that the NWO is secretly taking over everything is one shared by such disparate groups as UFO buffs and members of the right-wing militia movement.

One of the greatest mistakes that George Bush ever made during his term as president was to make a speech, at the conclusion of the Gulf War, in which he referred to a "New World Order" being established throughout the globe. Bush's obvious intention was to paint a rosy picture of ultimate peace, prosperity, and tranquility in a world where Soviet communism was a thing of the past and the USA was the predominant superpower. Unfortunately, the phrase evoked an unfortunate response in many people. For some it contained too many echoes of Hitler's "New Order" that he intended to establish after the defeat of Britain, the USA, and the Soviet Union. Others simply saw it as an over-enthusiastic confirmation of what many paranoid theorists had believed for years—a consortium of the richest and most powerful men, and the largest multinational corporations, was waiting in the wings for the right moment to make their move, ready to seize power after the ultimate collapse of democracy in the developed nations.

Researchers dug up a statement by Henry Kissinger allegedly made in the early 1970s: "Everything is going to be different. Many will suffer. A New World Order will emerge. It will be a much better world for those who survive. In the long run, life will be better. The world we have wanted will be reality." This could only add fuel to the flames already kindled by Bush. The militia/survivalist movement now saw even more reason to arm themselves and head for the woods. Apocalyptic Christian sects identified the NWO as the potential armies of the Antichrist and declared the biblical end of time to be upon us. Stories of black helicopters and mysterious concentration camp-style detention centers—manned by Turkish or Pakistani troops in UN uniforms—began to circulate on the fringes of the internet. Even in more logical circles, the fear was voiced that perhaps some repressive form of totalitarian world government could make a play for power in a situation when an energy crisis, climate disaster, widespread famine, and a shortage of industrial raw materials combined to threaten the underpinnings and basic systems of civilization.

The exact nature of the New World Order tends to vary according to which theorist one happens to be listening. The common threads and usual suspects are most often internationalist planning groups and think tanks. The Trilateral Commission, the Bilderburg Group, the Club of Rome, the Council for Foreign Affairs—any group that has made an in-depth study of the dangers of unchecked population growth and the dwindling of energy reserves has come under suspicion as being a NWO front organization. The more unchecked conspiracists will take it all the way back to the Vatican, international banking, and all the time-honored mystic secret societies already mentioned in Chapter 1.

A complete takeover

Although the professional paranoids may disagree as to the exact constituents of the New World Order, the basically American scenario for a takeover by NWO is reasonably consistent. The common fear is that a set of circumstances could arise in which the president (or in the event of the president's death, the vice president, the Speaker of the House, or whomever else might remain alive in the chain of command) could issue a directive

suspending the Constitution, revoking individual freedom, declaring martial law, and setting up a police state. With a consortium of Federal agencies assuming power, and the CIA and FBI acting as the spearhead enforcers, mass arrests would follow, along with total media censorship, while consumer goods—including food and energy—would be strictly rationed. This in turn would pave the way to complete takeover of the United States by the New World Order, and be a major stepping stone to a neo-fascist world government.

Fantastic? It certainly sounds like a grim science fiction synopsis, except that the mechanics for exactly this kind of revolution-from-the-top already exist in reality. In July 1984, the Knight-Ridder News Service broke the story of REX 84. Devised in the basement of the Reagan White House by Oliver North and National Guard Colonel Louis Giuffrida, REX 84 was a plan to "crush national opposition to any military action abroad" by "the suspension of the Constitution and the turning of control of the government over to FEMA (the Federal Emergency Management Agency)." According to columnist Jack Anderson, it also called for the "internment in concentration camps of up to 100,000 illegal immigrants and political dissidents" and would "clamp Americans in a totalitarian vice."

The seeds for REX 84 had originally been planted during the Kennedy administration when Executive Order 11051 provided for the temporary suspension of the Constitution and a declaration of martial law in the event of nuclear attack. The order was rewritten under Richard Nixon to make the same action possible in a number of national emergencies, and finally North and Giuffrida expanded it to be at the sole discretion of the president or any designated surrogate. Although the Iran-Contra investigations uncovered and sidetracked REX 84, its legal basis still remains on the books and, in the estimation of Professor Diana Reynolds of Northeastern University, "America is only a presidential directive away from a civil security state of emergency."

"WHAT DID THE PRESIDENT KNOW AND WHEN DID HE KNOW IT?"

Iran-Contra hearings, when his administration was accused of illegally channeling funds to the Contras. To all appearances, the Gipper knew nothing. While his people broke the law with eager deliberation, the president himself seemed happy to remain in blissful ignorance. The true relationship between Ronald Reagan and the CIA will now never be fully investigated or wholly revealed. Reagan has advanced Alzheimer's disease and Bill Casey conveniently took his secrets to the grave when he died of a brain tumor in 1987.

The fact that we may never know the truth about the CIA's true power in the 1980s even more strongly asks the question that if at least two presidents at the time could be excluded from the loop, and another could totally insulate himself from an entire progression of illegal covert operations, then who is really running the CIA and, by logical extension, who is really running the country?

The currency of drugs

If one single factor has consistently demonstrated how the CIA regards itself above and beyond the normal restrictions of both law and common morality, it has to be its 50-year involvement in international drug traffic. In Chapter 1 we saw how the French dockworkers were brought under political control when the CIA made a deal with the French Connection heroin importers. We also saw how the secret war in Laos and the more open conflict in Vietnam involved the granting of major concessions to the opium producers of the Golden Triangle. Later on in the book it will be shown how the agency, as a result of its bizarre experiments in brainwashing and mind control, almost single-handedly introduced LSD to the streets of the USA and the rest of the western world.

That the CIA should become involved with the sale and transportation of illegal drugs was, in some respects, almost inevitable. On one level, drugs—particularly heroin and cocaine—are the ideal method of moving money from one part of the world to another. Their weight-to-value ratio make them more easily packaged and more portable than anything other than uncut diamonds. Their very illegality means that they always retain their value. Unlike

52

left Cocaine is allegedly loaded onto a US-bound cargo plane at Los Brasiles airport in Nicaragua, supervised by Federico Vaughn, the "right-hand man" of Interior Minister Tomas Borge. This picture and others like it was used as a justification for aid to the Contras.

below *Parcels of US currency found in the office of Panama's Manuel Noriega.*

right *Manuel Noriega, when he was still the Company's golden boy.*

currency or even gold, they don't have to be processed through banks and are never subject to any serious market fluctuations. They cannot be traced, and covert channels of sales and distribution already exist and do not have to be created. In a situation where a nation's government or law enforcement is already tainted by corruption, narcotics are invariably the major stock in trade and means of exchange. From the point of view of any intelligence agency, drugs are simply too tempting a tool to be ignored. It also didn't help that three of the greatest areas of CIA involvement—Latin America, the Middle East, and South East Asia—are also the world's greatest producers of raw narcotics.

The very structure of the Company made the temptation of drug involvement extremely hard to resist. In organizations where the upper echelons—men like Allen Dulles, Richard Helms, and James Angleton—took the mandarin, almost contemptuous attitude that they were engaged in the Great Game, that they were warrior priests in the ideological, almost holy war against the communist "master plan" for world domination. The Agency was far above such mundane considerations as a proliferation of junkies and dealers on the streets of the country they were supposed to be protecting. They didn't even seem bothered by reports that, by 1969, one-third of the US combat troops in Vietnam were using heroin shipped from Laos via Thailand with the connivance of the CIA.

Tony (Poe) Posmepny

While Dulles, Helms, or Angleton occupied their ivory towers in Washington and Langley, the dirty work on the ground was being carried out by men like Tony (Poe) Posmepny—reputedly the model for the Marlon Brando character of Colonel Kurtz in Francis Ford Coppola's *Apocalypse Now*—the bluff and totally ruthless field controller who first ran the war in Laos and then moved on to special Phoenix operations in Vietnam. To men like Tony Poe, there was no greater objective than getting the job

done, fast and rough, with no moral niceties in the way. Damn the number of possibly innocent eggs that had to be broken to make the eventual omelet. When Tony Poe recruited the Laotian Mong tribesmen to fight the communist Pathet Lao and turned a blind eye to the fact that the Mong warlords' major source of income was from their crops of opium poppies, he set a pattern that would be repeated over and over in various locations during the next four decades.

In the years immediately after the Vietnam War, an almost exact rerun of the situation in Laos occurred in the Shan province of Burma, where supposedly anti-communist bandit leaders were given carte blanche to continue their production of opium. Through the 1970s and 1980s, the situation in Latin America became even more complicated. As cocaine became the fashionable drug of choice in Europe and America, countries like Peru, Colombia, Bolivia, Mexico, and Panama became so inundated with billions of dollars in drug money that it progressively ate away at the very foundations of their legal economies. By

DRUGS ARE SIMPLY TOO TEMPTING A TOOL TO BE IGNORED

the mid-1980s so much cocaine money had swamped Latin America that even conservatives like William F. Buckley began calling for an open debate on drug legalization. It was starting to look as though the money from the multi-billion dollar cocaine trade posed more of a potential danger than the drugs themselves.

In the same way that the proceeds from US alcohol prohibition in the roaring, speakeasy twenties provided the capital for organized crime to build up a proper structure, coke money was playing a major role in reshaping the political map of South and Central America. This was complemented by the unfortunate fact that much of the reshaping seemed to follow what was perceived as the Central Intelligence Agency's basic, long-term agenda to place the whole area under the control of repressive military regimes. A Congressional report in the early 1980s claimed that the police and military of no less than eight countries, including those mentioned above, plus Roberto d'Aubisson's Arena Party in El Salvador and the air force in Honduras, were all heavily involved in the cocaine trade. All of those mentioned had also received or were receiving substantial support from the CIA and other US agencies.

For a long time, the apex of this flourishing industry was the strategic transfer point in Panama. Under so-called "strong man" Manuel Noriega, most of the cocaine moving from Colombia and Bolivia up to consumers in the USA was channeled through Panama—with Noriega taking his cut and then moving the "merchandise" north, frequently with the cooperation and even the planes of the Mexican Air Force. Later, Noriega's arrogance became an irritant and then an embarrassment to the Bush administration, and George Bush sent troops to invade Panama and arrest Noriega in what has been dubbed by TV journalist Ted Koppel the "most expensive one man drug bust in history." But while Bush was head of the CIA and then vice president, Noriega was the poster boy for stalwart anti-communism, and the two men even had their picture taken together.

Oliver North and the Contras

The CIA's involvement in the cocaine trade came to a head during the Iran-Contra fiasco. Looking for any way to secretly aid the Contras in their goal of overthrowing Daniel Ortega and his leftist Sandinista regime in Nicaragua after the Boland Amendment had outlawed any direct financial support to the Contras, Oliver North at the White House and William Casey at the CIA happened upon a very simple source of covert revenue. By far the bulk of the weapons secretly being airlifted to the Contras were flown in ancient sub-contracted Honduran DC-6s. The flights were being coordinated by retired Air Force Major General Richard Secord—who, years earlier, had run the air support for Tony Poe's secret CIA war in Laos, and been instrumental in the instigation of Air America. Somewhere in the unholy trinity of North, Secord, and Casey, the realization seems to have dawned that all these DC-6s running weapons to the Contras were coming back empty and that was hardly cost-effective.

No record exists of who first had the idea of filling the old cargo planes with cocaine for the USA, but this is, without question, what happened. Pilot Fabio Carrasco confirms, on no less than four of the missions he flew, that

★
55
=

below *Oliver North testified in a uniform that he, in fact, no longer had the right to wear.*

right *His clients, the Contras. Nicaraguan cocaine paid for their arms.*

ARKANSAS, FULL CIRCLE

The following story was reported by no less than Norman Mailer. In the early 1980s, during the era of the Reagan administration's fear that Nicaraguan Sandinistas would destabilize Central America, turn it communist, and then invade Texas, some bright young men at the CIA decided to try to own and totally control a small Third World country. They felt they needed such a place as a permanent covert weapon system test facility and a central base for black operations. Their problem was they couldn't quite come up with a nation that had a sufficiently passive and docile indigenous population that they could rely on to remain that way in perpetuity, particularly if Company spooks were tearing up the landscape, mutilating cattle, and spraying the place with psychedelic nerve gas. Then an older hand interrupted. "Hell, boys," he told them, "you won't find anywhere more Third World than the Arkansas backwoods, and it's right here in the U.S. of A. All you need is a smart unscrupulous young governor to help you acquire the real estate. Of course, you might have to pay him off by helping him get to be president."

"weapons were removed and then quantities of coke in army bags were loaded onto the planes." With the "guns in/drugs out" policy of these Contra operations, the CIA finally crossed the line. The Company was no longer simply going along with the narcotics business, it was now actually running dope on its own account.

Clinton and the CIA

It will probably be some years before the real nature of the relationship between Bill Clinton and the CIA emerges. Through the Clinton administration, the CIA has been keeping something of a low profile. If it maintains its dreams of being a shadow government, it needs, at best, to be laying low, rebuilding its tarnished image, and gearing up for the 21st century. In addition to the damage created by the Iran-Contra revelations, the question remains whether the CIA actually has a role in the modern world without the specter of Soviet communism to justify its existence. Aspects of the Contra scandals constantly come

back to haunt the Agency. In 1997, CIA Director John Deutch was forced to confront an angry public meeting in South Central Los Angeles arranged by Congresswoman Maxine Waters to answer charges, made by reporter Gary Webb in the *San Jose Mercury News*, that, as part of the illegal financing of the Contras, the agency had been indirectly responsible for the supply of crack cocaine on the streets of the city's black and Hispanic neighborhoods. Deutch promised that the agency would conduct an extensive internal investigation, but his statement that the CIA would investigate itself was met with some derision.

The trouble with Afghanistan

Possibly the most dangerous legacy left by previous Company drug involvement is the current situation in Afghanistan. During the 1980s, after the Soviet invasion, the agency, working on the time-honored principle that "the enemies of our enemies are, by definition, our friends" had supplied the Afghan rebels—the Mujaheddin—with weapons and logistic support in their war against the Russians. The CIA had supplied the Mujaheddin with stinger missiles, capable of bringing down Russian helicopter gunships, and most military analysts agree that the action turned the tide of the Vietnam-style guerrilla

"ENEMIES OF OUR ENEMIES ARE, BY DEFINITION, OUR FRIENDS"

left The Mujaheddin; the CIA armed the Afghan fundamentalists for the guerrilla war against the Soviets, hardly considering that the same weapons might be turned against the USA in their Holy War against the Great Satan.

below *With the death of Colombian drug lord Pablo Escobar, power shifted to his rivals in the Cali Cartel who were already shipping Afghan heroin to the US.*

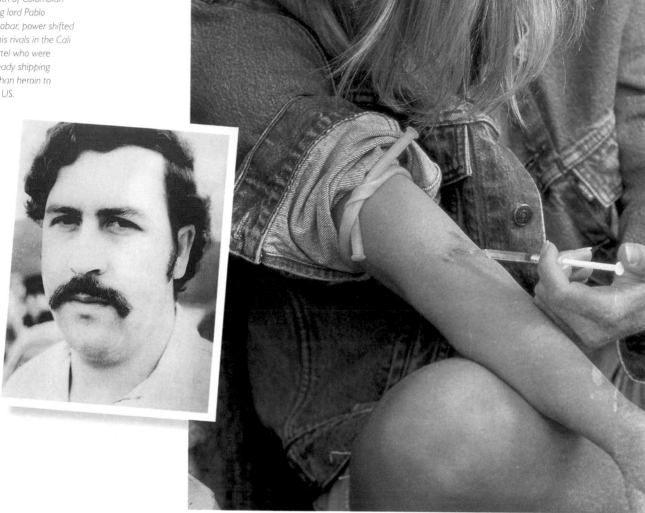

★
58
=

OPPOSED TO THE UNITED STATES AND ALL IT STOOD FOR

war and forced the Russian withdrawal. The Company involvement in Afghanistan didn't, however, come without its share of problems. Although the CIA support of the Mujaheddin may have achieved the immediate objective of inflicting a humiliating military defeat on the Red Army, it was short-sighted in so far as what might happen next. The Mujaheddin—although sworn enemies of the Soviet invaders—were also hardcore fundamentalist Moslems and implacably opposed to the United States and all it stood for.

Today, with an uneasy irony, the Mujaheddin, looking to both rebuild their country and continue the jihad against the US—the Great Satan—have turned huge areas of agricultural land over to the cultivation of opium that will ultimately arrive on the streets of the USA and Europe via the Colombian Cali Cartel, who have now diversified into heroin in addition to crack and cocaine. Adding more irony to the situation, the Cali Cartel are only in a position to do business with the Afghans because they had CIA support in their gang war with the rival Medellin Cartel. The Medellin Cartel was headed by the populist, left-leaning Pablo Escobar who, while certainly no saint, incurred the wrath of the Company by investing some of his drug profits in low cost public housing and by maintaining a tentative relationship with Castro. The CIA almost certainly had an advisory role in his surrender to the Colombian authorities and his subsequent death "while trying to escape."

THE CIA IN SPACE

The ultimate conspiracy theory, surpassing even that of the CIA and the New World Order, has, of course, to be the idea that the CIA is not only the enforcement arm of some totalitarian government in waiting, but—via a deeply mysterious group known as MJ12—is actually working with extraterrestrials from another star system toward their ultimate colonization of the Earth. The highly advanced aliens have seemingly made a pliable cross section of world leaders—including the heads of the CIA—an offer they couldn't refuse. In an alien-run slave state, with the ultimate goal of crossbreeding human-alien worker hybrids, MJ12 and its followers could maintain power and privilege during their lifetimes, providing they pledged total loyalty to the ET overlords.

The scenario of the CIA being involved with extraterrestrials goes all the way back to the earliest days of the Agency. As the story is told by the CIA/UFO conspiracy theorists like William Cooper, and the infamous Commander X, author of *The Cosmic Patriot Files*, after the crash of one UFO in Aztec, Nevada and another near White Sands Proving Ground, the primary missile test site of the time, a total of 17 extraterrestrial bodies were recovered from these wrecks. Then a live alien was discovered wandering in the desert after a slightly later crash at Roswell. A security clampdown, more complete than the one imposed on the Manhattan Project and the development of the atom bomb, was organized by a combination of the CIA and the air force.

In 1951, the surviving ET became ill, and with human doctors baffled, it was allowed to phone home. The aliens arrived three years later. Their first landing took place in a remote desert location and, in fact, the film *Close Encounters Of The Third Kind* is a thinly-fictionalized version of the actual event. After this initial contact, the aliens arrived in force, landed at Muroc (now Edwards) Air Force Base, and met with President Dwight Eisenhower. Recognizing that humanity didn't stand a chance against the highly advanced ETs, Eisenhower essentially negotiated a conditional surrender of humanity whereby the CIA—taking their orders from MJ12 and the NWO—would gradually prepare the Earth for colonization. A few days later, Eisenhower suffered a non-fatal heart attack. All that has happened since has been a direct result of this secret alien infiltration.

The story is, of course, fantastic. The problem with immediately dismissing it as laughable is that it's set in a world where the fantastic has been proved, over and over again, to be no laughing matter.

59

right *Hangar 18 at Wright Patterson Air Force Base where aliens' bodies are alleged to be stored, and (inset) the Roswell UFO crash site.*

CHAPTER THREE

THE CIA'S GREATEST HITS

Executive Actions that Changed the World

Almost all of those who use murder as part of their stock in trade have particular euphemisms for the act of killing. In the Mob, professional assassins talk about someone being "whacked" or call a killing a "hit." Among the grunts in Vietnam the popular word was "greased." The KGB under Stalin tended to "eliminate" their real or supposed enemies. At CIA headquarters in Langley, the most often used phrases were "executive action" and the even more chilling "terminated with extreme prejudice." An individual who could be counted on to kill was considered an "asset." The very terminology says much about the CIA mindset. Where the hitmen of organized crime used words that tended to minimize their actions, to make a killing seem almost mundane, a joke, certainly a matter of no great importance, the CIA agent hid the true reality of what he or she was doing behind a screen of quasi-corporate jargon. To arrange and plan the death of another human being is presented as a matter of cool detachment. Assassination is merely another instrument of policy, a means of achieving a desired goal. The killing of an enemy is reduced to the level of exercising a stock option or putting together a leveraged buyout. It's little wonder that the CIA has always liked to refer to itself as "the Company."

facing page *In at the death (clockwise from top left): Revolutionary and guerrilla fighter Che Guevara; Congolese Prime Minister Patrice Lumumba; party girl Vicki Morgan; Muslim leader Malcolm X. The CIA has been implicated, or at least suspected, in all of their deaths.*

below *Suspicions remain that the CIA, or at least a rogue group within the Company, may have been behind the assassination of John F. Kennedy.*

★

61

A bag of ears

Only now and then, and usually in times of extreme stress, does the realization come to the fore that what is being done is the deliberate murder of another human being. During Operation Phoenix in Vietnam, CIA headquarters became obsessed with the idea of the daily "body count" being an accurate quantitative measure of the program's effectiveness. When legendary field operative Tony (Poe) Posmepny was questioned by the upper echelons in Saigon regarding the accuracy of his body count reports, his response was immediately to dispatch a courier with a bag of Viet Cong ears to the Vietnamese capital. Tony Poe prided himself on the fact that the one thing he knew how to do efficiently and with numerical accuracy was to kill the enemy. The ears in question were all left ears, just to ensure that his superiors understood that he wasn't in any way trying to pad the numbers and claim a doubled kill ratio.

A COURIER WITH A BAG OF VIET CONG EARS

For the most part, however, detachment has always been the hallmark of CIA assassinations. Where a crime boss or drug lord might order an execution as a matter of revenge, punishment for a supposed infraction, or as a public example to keep others in line, the CIA almost always kills as a part of what it sees as the big picture. CIA death sentences are rarely carried out from a motivation of payback. When an individual is removed, it is almost always because she or he poses a threat to the Company world view, or because that individual is seen as being engaged in a course of action that is in opposition to what the Agency deems to be the national interest.

In terms of methodology, the CIA has always gone the metaphoric route of night and fog. Unlike the Mafia, where the tacit understanding of who whacked whom has always remained fairly clear as an unequivocal message to the opposition, the CIA—although the message is clearly sent and the irritant or impediment removed—allows the details of the hit to remain, as far as possible, shrouded in mystery. The key to understanding how the CIA generally goes about its "wet work" is the phrase "plausible deniability." It must be known that the CIA was behind the killing. The enemy has to know that the Company had terminated their man with "extreme prejudice," but the Agency also needs to be able to smile blandly and deny the

MURDER ACADEMY

The use of torture to obtain confessions or otherwise induce individuals to make statements or perform acts that they wouldn't countenance under normal circumstances has been largely outlawed by most civilized countries as being both morally repugnant and practically ineffective. The former hardly needs any clarification, and the latter is neatly summed up in an a CIA document from the early 1950s that excludes the use of torture because of its "dubious effectiveness as compared with various supplemental psychoanalytical techniques." Or, as one field operative more bluntly put it: "You can blowtorch a man's ass, but he'll only tell you what you want to hear." Despite these reservations, evidence abounds that the CIA more than once applied the metaphoric blowtorch and also the not-so-metaphoric bullet in the back of the head, and even taught the more refined techniques of murder and torture to military and law enforcement officials of client countries, first at the International Police Academy in Los Fresnos, Texas, and later at the notorious School of the Americas at Fort Benning, Georgia.

The curriculum at the School of the Americas—essentially based on the savage Phoenix Program used in Vietnam, but modified for primary use in Latin America—provides a horrific blueprint for the conversion of any medium sized nation into a ruthlessly aggressive police state by means of repression, control, intimidation, and execution. The end result is a society so diametrically opposed to the professed US ideals of freedom and justice for all that the CIA's ultimate goal must once again be questioned. One of the School's primary textbooks that has become public in recent years is The CIA Interrogation Manual. Although the book concentrates on the psychological techniques for breaking down a subject, it is implicit that the described intimidation and disorientation may be used—in combination with drugs—as adjuncts to physical torture, such as beating, burning, electric shock, partial drowning, sleep deprivation, and rape:

"The ideal time to make an arrest is in the early hours of the morning. When arrested at this time, most subjects experience intense feelings of shock, insecurity and psychological stress."

As arrest moves to incarceration and actual questioning, the instructions in the manual become increasingly grim:

"The subject must be convinced that his 'questioner' controls his ultimate destiny and that his absolute cooperation is necessary for his survival."

That the manual sees the psychological softening up only as a prelude to worse suffering is hardly disguised:

"A threat should be delivered coldly, not shouted in anger. When a threat is used, it should always be implied that the subject himself is to blame. 'You leave me no other choice but to...' If a subject refuses to comply after a threat is made, it must be carried out. If it is not carried out, then other threats become meaningless."

A second manual—issued to the Nicaraguan Contras under the title *The CIA Freedom Fighters' Manual*—goes a stage further and covers the subject of death squads. It stresses that although the fiction must be maintained that a death squad—a murder unit with the specific task of eliminating suspected political undesirables— although usually composed of either off-duty police or military, must have no visible connection with the ruling authority. At the same time, however, it has to be known that it was the fatal vengeance of that same authority that instigated the killings. In Vietnam, the Phoenix squads left Ace of Spades calling cards beside the bodies of their suspected VC victims. Under various Latin American regimes, the death squads would make themselves known by all driving a particular make and model of car. In the 1960s, the Ford Falcon was the car of

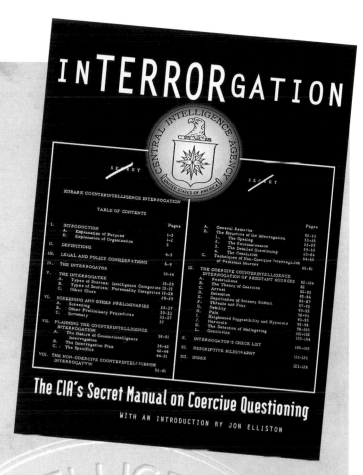

InTERRORgATION

The CIA's Secret Manual on Coercive Questioning

WITH AN INTRODUCTION BY JON ELLISTON

★

63

choice, but by the 1980s it had been replaced by the Jeep Cherokee. In El Salvador, the death squads of Roberto D'Aubuisson wore black Oakland Raiders T-shirts as unofficial uniforms.

In the Spring 1994 edition of *Covert Action Quarterly*, writer Clyde Snow describes how the CIA/School of the Americas-trained death squads operated in Guatemala during the 1970s and 1980s. "An informer with a hooded face accompanies police along a city street, pointing people out: who shall live and who shall die... 'this one's a son of a bitch'... 'that one'... anyone with a vaguely leftist political association or moderate criticism of government policy. Men [are] found with their eyes gouged out, their testicles in their mouths, without hands or tongues, women with their breasts cut off." If it starts to sound as though the School of the Americas is a training ground for homicidal sadists, Clyde Snow leaves us in no doubt: "The military guys who do this are like serial killers. If Jeffrey Dahmer had been in Guatemala he would be a general by now."

whole thing in front of press and TV. As we saw in the previous chapter, the one thing the Company has always feared, almost as much as communism, is an unfettered and uncontrolled press.

After a CIA assassination, the water always had to be sufficiently muddy so that the upper echelons could walk away, if not smelling sweet, then at least with no smoking gun connected to them. In overseas operations, one of the first ways to divorce the Company from its homicides was, wherever and whenever possible, to use the locals. Regardless of whether the target was a prominent figure like Patrice Lumumba or Che Guevara, or just one of the body count in a serial campaign of rank and file death and terror, the CIA always preferred to recruit local gangsters, law enforcement, military, or a group of hired defectors, to do the actual deed. CIA operatives might plan the hit, supply the weapons and the cash, and facilitate the getaway. They might even be present at the execution, but as long as someone else pulled the trigger, then it was possible to issue a statement to the effect that the murder or murders were a result of "the locals getting overzealous" and efforts would be made to ensure that "nothing like it happened again."

When, however, as during the Johnson, Nixon, and Reagan administrations, the Company knows that it has the total backing of the White House, the denials can become almost contemptuous, pushing the envelope of plausibility almost until it tears. In 1980, a bus carrying a group of seven nuns of the progressive Maryknoll Order doing medical missionary work in strife-torn El Salvador was ambushed by a right-wing military death squad. After autopsies proved the nuns had been raped and then shot, a CIA spokesmen attempted to excuse the actions of his supposed political allies by claiming that the soldiers opened fire because the nuns "might have been carrying weapons." The image of armed nuns would almost have a Monty-Python-like humor but for the horror of the actual context, and it clearly demonstrated that, at the time, the Agency seemed to believe that it could get away with pretty much anything.

above *Patrice Lumumba. The Agency was not prepared to tolerate him looking to the USSR for support.*

right *American Maryknoll nun Rita Ford is buried after her alleged murder by a Salvadoran death squad.*

The killing of Patrice Lumumba

The death of Patrice Lumumba in the early 1960s is a classic example of a particular kind of CIA assassination in which the signal is sent, but the details remain, for all time, less than clear. In 1960, the Belgians had pulled out their African colony in the Congo, leaving chaos and instability behind. The former Belgian Congo was a vital source of minerals for America and Western Europe, and the fear in Washington was that Moscow might attempt to establish a satellite government there as it had previously done in Poland, Hungary, and other parts of Eastern Europe. For the Soviet bloc to extend itself to Africa was absolutely unthinkable. To the Dulles brothers' mindset, the Reds had half Europe and they also had China. If they established a foothold in Africa, it could only be the beginning of the end for freedom and democracy. At all cost, they had to be stopped, and the Belgians weren't being particularly helpful by backing

left *The CIA-approved murder of South Vietnamese President Ngo Dinh Diem was a major factor in turning JFK against the war.*

THE CIA WALKED AWAY WITH NO PROVABLE INVOLVEMENT

Lumumba's arch rival, General Moise Tshombe, in the establishment of the copper-rich Katanga province as a separate independent state.

When UN troops had failed to contain Tshombe's army of native troops and South African and European "Wild Geese" mercenaries, Lumumba had appealed to the USSR for help. In that move, he had sealed his fate. Although Lumumba would shortly be ousted from the Congolese premiership, the Company still believed that it would be safer to kill him before he could stage a political comeback. No less an agent than Dr. Sydney Gottlieb, the head of the Agency's super secret MKULTRA chemical weapons division, arrived in the capital, Leopoldville, with a selection of untraceable bio-toxins to use on Lumumba. As it turned out, Dr. Gottlieb's services would not, in the end, be needed. With CIA connivance, Lumumba was betrayed to Tshombe's forces and murdered while in captivity. Although rumor was rife, the CIA walked away with no provable involvement in the death of the African leader, and the Congo was now set on a course to have its name changed to Zaire and, under the dictatorship of Dulles' favorite, Joseph Mobutu, to suffer three long decades of one of the most corrupt regimes in all of black Africa.

Ngo Dinh Diem is terminated

Two years later, in 1963, another head of state would be "terminated with prejudice." In South Vietnam, President Ngo Dinh Diem was proving to be something of an embarrassment. At the same time as constantly demanding increases in American military aid to fight the communists in the north, his promised political reforms weren't forthcoming and, worse still, Diem's Catholic regime was conducting a brutally and openly repressive campaign against its Buddhist opposition. President Kennedy, looking to downscale US involvement in Vietnam—as he put it in a TV interview, "it's their war"—was not keen on forcibly removing Diem, but the Company thought otherwise.

On November 1st, 1963, with full backing of the CIA in Saigon, a group of generals seized power and murdered Diem. Kennedy was not informed of the coup until after the fact. Lyndon Johnson recalled that permission for the action was approved by mid-level State Department officials during a weekend when "Jack Kennedy was off in a sailboat at Hyannis and Dean Rusk was away." Kennedy was furious. He may have been weary of Diem, but he hadn't wanted him murdered, particularly as the story was circulating that a ranking CIA official was present. His resolve was stiffened to "bring Americans out of there," but just three weeks later he would be gunned down.

LN 488435

HOW/SAL

LONG

MERCENARIES IN ACTION

BOENDE; CONGO REPUBLIC :" WHITE MERCENARIES; FIGHTING
WITH REGULAR CONGOLESE ARMY TROOPS AGAINST THE CONGOLESE
REBELS, IN ACTION DURING THE ATTACK ON BOENDE, A "KEY"
POINT FOR THE ADVANCE ON STANLEYVILLE, ON OCTOBER 23RD
AFTER SEVERAL WEEKS OF HARD FIGHTING, BOENDE FELL ON
OCTOBER 24TH, WITHOUT A SHOT BEING FIRED. ACCORDING
TO REPORTS, THE TOWN FELL AFTER REBEL RESISTANCE WAS
BROKEN BY AIR RAIDS BY THE WHITE-PILOTED CONGO AIR FORCE

13TH NOVEMBER 1964 PN-HB

UNITED PRESS INTERNATIONAL

right *Mercenaries fighting in the Congo. Actions like this sowed the seeds of the Soldier of Fortune/Wild Geese mythology.*

below *Mad Mike Hoare, the ex-British paratrooper who led the mercenary forces in the Congo.*

66

On the trail of Che Guevara

Although Ernesto "Che" Guevara wasn't a head of state, he was, as far as CIA assassination operations went, one of their major scores. As a founder of the Cuban revolution and Fidel Castro's right-hand man, the charismatic, Argentinean-born guerrilla fighter and Marxist idealist had been a thorn in the CIA's side ever since Castro had come to power, and it was little wonder that, when Che was wounded and captured by Bolivian Rangers and their Green Beret/CIA advisors, they gathered around him like big game hunters around a prize kill. He had even been given the

target codename AMQUACK, referring to the fact that he was a qualified doctor.

With one of the bizarre ironies that seem to dog the history of the Company, it was the CIA itself that had actually set Che Guevara on the path that would bring him to the number two spot in the Cuban power structure and also to his death, seven years later in Bolivia. After graduating from medical school in Argentina, Che and a friend, Alberto Granado, traveled the length of South America on an ancient Norton motorcycle, like a couple of Latin beatniks. Granado would eventually return to Buenos Aires, but Che had a need to continue his wanderings and eventually wound up in Guatemala City at the very moment the CIA was overthrowing the leftist Arbenz government. Working as an emergency medic during the bombing of the city by CIA pilots seems to have crystallized Guevara's revolutionary politics and his contempt for the US power structure and its profit-driven goals.

Che Guevara would sail on the yacht *Grandma* with Castro as part of the ill-fated invasion force that would all but be wiped out immediately after they landed in Cuba. He would fight in the Sierra Maestra mountains while Castro rebuilt his strength, and ride into Havana in triumph after

right *Officers of the elite Bolivian Rangers display the body of Che Guevara like a trophy. (inset) Bolivian Government propaganda poster.*

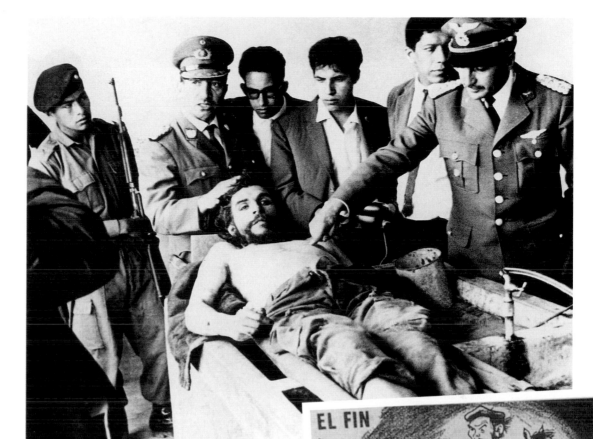

EL FIN

DEL "CHE"

the fall of the Batista regime. Guevara found it hard, however, to settle to the routine business of running a country. In the comparative calm after the desperate days of the Bay of Pigs and the Cuban Missile Crisis, the perpetually footloose Guevara spent time as a traveling ambassador for the new Cuban government, but then, chafing under the increasing Soviet grip on the way Cuba was being managed, decided to take his revolution elsewhere and return to his old trade of guerrilla fighter.

He fought against Tshombe and the white mercenaries under "Mad" Mike Hoare in the Congo, but although he found himself on the losing side in this conflict, the Company saw him as a dangerous adversary and promoted him to the top of their hit list, directly below Fidel himself. In some respects, Guevara was a symbol of the Agency's worst nightmare, embodying the idea of the wandering exporter of the communist "disease." After the defeat in the Congo, Che returned to Cuba, but again clashed with the Soviet officials who were calling the shots. His sights then turned on Bolivia, where the copper miners—who were crucial to the country's economy—were in almost open conflict with the military regime of General Rene Barrientos. Guevara not only wanted to unseat the military

junta, but, since Bolivia was the geographic heart of South America—sharing common borders with seven other countries—he saw it as the strategic springboard to a Pan American revolution.

Needless to say, at Langley the motivation to see Guevara dead now developed critical mass, although, in some respects, the Agency fell victim to its own propaganda in the furious determination that it went after Guevara. The truth was that the threat posed to Barrientos and Bolivia by Che Guevara and his small force of Cubans was more symbolic than actual and, in virtual confirmation of this, the revolutionary campaign began to become

THE MAN WHO KILLED CHE

Felix Rodriguez, the CIA agent who is credited with the capture and killing of Che Guevara, had a similar dedication to the Company and counter revolution as his adversary had to the overthrow of capitalism. Rodriguez's uncle had been Batista's Minister of Works in prerevolutionary Cuba, and when Castro took over, the Rodriguez family were forced into exile. Embittered by this misfortune, Rodriguez went to the Dominican Republic and joined the CIA-backed Anti-Communist Legion that was planning an invasion of Cuba. When the invasion force left, Rodriguez was not included. Although—since the invasion was an even worse failure than the Bay of Pigs—being left behind saved Rodriguez from either death or a long imprisonment in a Cuban jail, the angry 19 year old vowed to dedicate his life to the overthrow of Castro. He joined Brigade 2506, training in Guatemala for yet another invasion, graduated to one of the CIA "Grey Teams" making hit and run sabotage attacks in the Cuban countryside, and was actually in Havana when the Bay of Pigs landing took place.

Following the Bay of Pigs fiasco, Rodriguez would join Operation Mongoose, plotting the murder of Fidel Castro. His specific task was to go inside Cuba and set up counter-revolutionary lines of communication. After Mongoose failed to achieve its objective, he returned to work out of the Miami field office, where he would get the call to join the hunt for Che Guevara in Bolivia. After the death of Che, he moved on to take part in operations in Vietnam, El Salvador, and other war-torn countries. He worked as Oliver North's pointman in the supply of illegal aid to the Contras. When his cover was blown by the Iran-Contra hearings, he was forced to retire to a secluded suburb of Miami, where he still lives.

seriously unglued. Supplies from Cuba mysteriously dried up, Che fell out with the local Bolivian Communist Party, and then made a tactical error that would lead directly to his death. Instead of joining the miners in the more urban areas, Che tried to reproduce the way that the Cuban revolution had been fought. He took to the mountains and high jungles but, instead of finding the peasants joining him in a spontaneous uprising, he and his tall, bearded Cubans scared the hell out of the predominantly Indian population, who were afraid even to sell food to him and his men for fear of Government reprisals. Bolivia had been plagued by foreign bandits and adventurers since the days of Butch Cassidy and the Sundance Kid, and many of the mountain people assumed that Che and his men were simply more of the same.

Despite the fact that Guevara seemed to be messing up all on his own, a combined force of some 3000 Bolivian Rangers—specially trained in counter-insurgency—plus American CIA agents and a detachment of Green Berets, was sent into the mountains to hunt down Guevara. On October 8th, 1967, after a prolonged firefight near the mountain hamlet of La Higuera, Che was wounded and captured. Although various accounts differ, it would seem that, once they knew Guevara had been taken alive, the CIA wanted to keep him that way, to debrief, to interrogate, maybe to put on trial and certainly to show him to the world as proof that this was not some communist superman. According to CIA agent Felix Rodriguez, who talked with Guevara through the single night that he was a prisoner, it was the Bolivians who gave the order and made sure that Guevara was shot to death a little before dawn.

This laying off the blame for Che's death may have

ALL THAT THE PUBLIC EVER HEARS IS RUMOR

been, in part, a face-saving exercise. As a propaganda coup, the killing of Che Guevara backfired globally on the CIA. Within days of his death, his charisma and good looks made him a world wide icon. His image instantly appeared on T-shirts and posters in bohemian enclaves from New York to Tokyo. His image was carried by everyone from striking grape pickers in Southern California to radical students in Paris. Even today his image recurs, as when the rock band Rage Against The Machine used it on the cover of their CD "Face." By killing Che Guevara, the Agency had quite literally created the poster boy for the 1960s revolution.

The violent death of Malcolm X

Not all CIA assassinations take place in the deepest jungle or under cover of a Third World country in the chaotic throes of a civil war. When they happen in a supposedly more civilized location, however, the plausible deniability has to be many notches tighter and, frequently, all that the public ever hears is rumor and speculation. No direct evidence has ever been presented, for instance, that the CIA had any hand in the death of militant black leader Malcolm X, but suspicions of CIA involvement have

persisted. On February 21st, 1965, Malcolm—who described himself as a former "hoodlum, dope-peddler, and pimp," but who had risen to the level of militant international spokesman for African Americans—took the stage to address a meeting in the Audubon Ballroom in New York City. Before he could say a word, though, he was hit in the chest by a blast from a sawn-off shotgun. According to a 1967 article in *The Realist*, "all eyewitness reports...indicated a total of five gunmen had been involved, but only one, Thomas Hagen, was caught."

Hagen turned out to be a member of Elijah Mohammed's Nation of Islam. Since Malcolm had spilt with Elijah Mohammed a year earlier, after being a prominent and devoted disciple, to set up his own group—the Organization of Afro-American Unity—it was assumed that the killing was a matter of sectarian revenge. Many prominent blacks, however, thought differently. Congress for Racial Equality National Director James Ferguson told the *New York Times*: "the killing of Malcolm X was a political act, with international implications."

For many, "international implications" meant the CIA. Prior to his death, Malcolm couldn't help but have come to the Agency's attention when he went on a world tour and was accorded virtual ambassador status in countries like

Ghana, Egypt, and Saudi Arabia. His open condemnation of the US involvement in the Congo must also have not endeared him to the Company. A further pointer was that during the tour, the day before he was due to address a summit conference of African prime ministers in Cairo, he collapsed with severe stomach pains after eating dinner in the Cairo Hilton. After being rushed to hospital, Malcolm's stomach was pumped out and, according to medical reports, a "toxic substance was found and natural food poisoning was ruled out." Malcolm himself suspected the CIA. Later, on the same tour, he was refused permission to enter France, and stories spread that the French Department of Alien Documentation and Counter Espionage had learned that the CIA had a contract out on Malcolm X and wanted to make sure the hit didn't take place on French soil.

As far as those who believe the Agency organized Malcolm's death are concerned, the circumstantial evidence continued to pile up. A few days before the deadly shooting, Malcolm's home in Queens was fire bombed, and three weeks after Malcolm was killed, his acting successor in the OAAU, Leon Ameer announced: "I have facts in my possession as to who really killed Malcolm X. The killers aren't from Chicago [Muslim headquarters]. They're from Washington." Ameer was scheduled to give a press conference at which he would present these "facts," including documents and tape recordings. The press conference never happened; the next morning, Ameer was found dead in Boston's Sherry Biltmore Hotel. The police reported that he had died of an "epileptic fit," but his wife contended he had no medical history of epilepsy.

The assassination of the century

Perhaps the idea that the CIA had terminated Malcolm X—with Thomas Hagen being used as the patsy or fall guy—might not have lingered so long if it hadn't carried so many echoes of what might arguably be called the greatest assassination of the 20th century. Part of the split between Malcolm X and Elijah Mohammed was caused by a speech that Malcolm made immediately after the murder of President John Kennedy, when he grimly observed that "the chickens were coming home to roost." Elijah Mohammed, feeling that the statement could only do harm to the Muslim

right *The President's motorcade moves through Dallas to its terrible date with destiny.*

below *Lee Harvey Oswald shows off his guns, but was the picture faked? Photographic experts, after studying the shadow patterns, claim the head is Oswald's but that it is montaged onto a different body.*

70

72

THREE MAJOR SUSPECTS: THE FBI, THE CIA, AND THE MAFIA

cause, suspended Malcolm from official speaking and the rift began. This piece of spin control, however, couldn't stop the death of Malcolm X from being inexorably linked with the JFK shooting and the other high profile assassinations that would follow, most notably those of Bobby Kennedy and Martin Luther King Jr.

In any study of the CIA and its use of assassination as an instrument of policy, the big question that can never be avoided is: Did the Company have a hand in the murder of John Fitzgerald Kennedy? Enough books have been written about the Kennedy assassination to fill a medium-sized library, and we do not have the space here to analyze the volumes of evidence, both actual and anecdotal, to make the case either for or against. Suffice to say that more than two thirds of the American people do not believe the findings of the hastily convened Warren Commission that Lee Harvey Oswald was the lone gunman shooting in Dealey Plaza on November 22nd, 1963. The moment that

Oswald acting alone is removed from the equation, the CIA very definitely becomes a contender.

The overwhelming bulk of the material that has been published on the Kennedy murder presents us with three major suspects: the FBI, the CIA, and the Mafia. In nearly all of the theories, both reasoned and paranoid, only the two agencies, or organized crime at its most highly organized, would have had the assets and resources not only to plan and execute the killing of the President of the United States, in a public place, in broad daylight, and get away with it, but also to conduct a cover up that involved the destruction of records on the highest level and the murder of over 50 people.

The case against the Mafia

Logic would dictate that the Mafia can probably be dropped from the trio of suspects fairly early in the game. The Mob in general, and Sam Giancana in particular, felt bitter that, in their estimation, they had come through for Joseph Kennedy when he called in markers from his rum-running prohibition days during his son's 1960 election bid. Mob figures, including Giancana, had thrown their not inconsiderable influence and connections behind helping his son win the 1960 presidential election against Richard Nixon, only to have the Kennedys turn on them when they came to power.

No sooner had JFK appointed his brother Robert to the post of Attorney General than he started a highly publicized vendetta against organized crime, going after Jimmy Hoffa and the Teamsters Union, a crucial source of Mob funds and its principal money laundering facility. If that wasn't bad enough, the failure of the Bay of Pigs had dashed all hopes of men like Meyer Lansky and Carlos Marcello of reclaiming their holdings in Cuba, and they blamed the failure on John Kennedy's perceived betrayal of the operation. The Mob definitely had a motive, but whether they had the means or opportunity is another matter. The complexity of the conspiracy needed to shoot the president and then hang the rap on Lee Oswald would seem to be way beyond even Mafia capabilities, unless its role was in

right *Lee Harvey Oswald is killed by one-time mob hitman Jack Ruby, live on world TV, in the basement of Dallas Police HQ. Assassin or patsy?*

below *J. Edgar Hoover; a major conspiracy to kill the president could hardly have proceeded without his knowledge.*

tandem with one of the other two candidates. On its own, the Mob simply does not have the contacts, clout, and know-how to shred secret files of government agencies and, for example, take down the Washington telephone system for a full hour as happened on the afternoon of the assassination. At best, the Mob could only have played a back-up role, conceivably organizing some of the post-assassination clean-up, starting with Jack Ruby's shooting of Oswald.

The case against the FBI

Although it would have to have participated in the cover-up after the fact, the FBI can also be ruled out as a part of any deliberate conspiracy to kill the president. Although longtime FBI Director J. Edgar Hoover loathed both Jack and Bobby Kennedy, he certainly had enough in his files on Jack, as a result of the president's compulsive womanizing, to have little need to kill him. Blackmail would have more easily served Hoover's purpose. This is not to say that, through his extensive domestic spy network, he didn't hear about the plot and let it roll ahead under its own momentum, but both logic and the odds would indicate that the FBI played no active part until afterward.

above *Seconds after the shooting, a Secret Service agent jumps onto Kennedy's speeding car.*

★
74
=

The finger points to the CIA

This irrevocably leads us to the CIA. In terms of the three classic tests of any criminal investigation, the Agency had the motive, the means, and the opportunity. As far as the Company was concerned, JFK had three strikes against him. He had called their bluff over the Bay of Pigs and refused to be blackmailed into committing US air and ground support, he was seriously considering pulling the US out of Vietnam and putting a stop to the Company's handy little war and, worst of all, he had threatened to tear down the CIA itself.

Once emotion and paranoia are put to one side, even the murder itself takes on the look of a CIA termination. President Kennedy was shot to death during a routine,

THE FINGER-PRINTS OF THE CIA WOULD SEEM TO BE ALL OVER THE STORY

show-himself-to-the-people electioneering motorcade in Dallas, Texas. At the last minute, the route of the motorcade was changed so it would pass through the open area of Dealey Plaza, where the president was killed by shots to the head and upper body, fired by—according to eyewitnesses and the home movie made by Abraham Zapruder—at least two gunmen with highly accurate, high-powered rifles, firing from at least two

LEE HARVEY OSWALD

The Oswald story is, to put it mildly, somewhat murky. A kid from a broken home, with an uncle who worked for mobster Carlos Marcello, he enlisted in the Marines and was assigned to a secret base in Japan where U2 spy flights were launched. He became a Marxist and defected to Russia. He became disillusioned with communism and returned to the USA with his Russian wife. While appearing to support Castro with his one-man Fair Play For Cuba committee, he also maintained relationships with right-wing extremists and known CIA operatives. He was arrested within hours of the shooting and subsequently killed. Although reputedly a lousy shot, the Warren Commission hung the whole deal on him and the world's collective consciousness boggled. Conspiracy theories instantly abounded and, in the majority, Oswald was assigned the role of the CIA-programmed "patsy," something he himself claimed in a brief moment on camera after his arrest.

JACK RUBY

Jack Ruby, a.k.a. Jack Rubenstein, had no direct ties to the CIA, but was a small-time crook from way back. In 1963, he was a lower echelon strip

club operator and fixer in Dallas. In his younger days in Chicago, though, evidence suggests that he might have carried out hits for Jimmy Hoffa. If the Mob were running the JFK cleanup for the CIA, Ruby would have been the ideal gunman to "ice the patsy."

E. HOWARD HUNT

E. Howard Hunt turns up all over the map of CIA covert ops. The dirtier the job, the more likely Hunt is to be there. He worked operations in Guatemala, against Castro, and later he would loom large in Watergate. Attorney Mark Lane, in his book *Plausible Denial*, accused Hunt of being the CIA paymaster for the Kennedy assassination. Hunt sued for libel, but lost his case.

GENERAL CHARLES CABELL

Charles Cabell was Assistant Director of the CIA until fired by President Kennedy after the Bay of Pigs. His brother Earl was the mayor of Dallas at the time of the assassination. He was the one who changed the motorcade route so it made the slow, fatal turn past the Texas Book Depository.

CLAY SHAW

When Clay Shaw (top left) was prosecuted by New Orleans District Attorney Jim Garrison (below left) as a conspirator in the murder of JFK, the Agency denied that he had ever worked for them. Later, when pressed, it admitted that he was one of their operatives. Warren Commission supporters like to point to fact that a jury acquitted Shaw. It must be noted, though, that the same jury did go on record as believing a conspiracy did take place in the murder of the president, but that Garrison had failed to produce enough evidence to tie Clay Shaw to it and secure a conviction.

GUY BANNISTER

Ex-FBI agent Guy Bannister was supposedly training Cuban exiles for covert CIA missions into Cuba when he employed Lee Oswald during the summer of 1963.

DAVID FERRIE

One of the weirdest characters in the JFK conspiracy files, David Ferrie was gay, unstable, totally lacking in head or body hair, and an expert pilot. He worked for the CIA under Guy Bannister, flying covert missions into Cuba. A few days after being named by Jim Garrison—along with Clay Shaw—as being one of the JFK conspirators, he died under mysterious circumstances, effectively wrecking Garrison's case against Shaw.

DR. LOUIS WEST

The mysterious Dr. West was a pioneer of LSD research for the CIA and reputedly killed an elephant by giving it 300,000 micrograms of acid. While Jack Ruby was in prison, West attended him and declared that Ruby was suffering from "delusions" that the USA was being taken over by a "fascist plot."

RICHARD NIXON

By the oddest of chances, Richard Nixon was in Dallas on the day of the assassination, supposedly on business for Pepsi Cola.

above *Bobby Kennedy is shot by the possibly brainwashed Sirhan Sirhan.*
centre *Martin Luther King Jr. is also shot in the same year with similar questions about alleged assassin James Earl Ray.*
right *Paranoia reached such proportions that some believed the Company might have tried to silence Bob Dylan by setting him up for a motorcycle accident.*

positions in the area. Prior to the shooting, the Secret Service protection had become noticeably lax, without the usual routine checks being made on open windows overlooking the route. Afterwards a "lone gunman" was swiftly arrested but killed in police custody by an assassin with connections to the Mob. The suspect was apparently interrogated at some length, but no notes were kept. In the months and years following the crime, close to 60 people— either witnesses or individuals connected with some phase of the operation—died in mysterious circumstances. The fingerprints of the CIA, or at least a renegade group inside the Agency, would seem to be all over the story, and yet the debate continues.

Conspiracy theories multiply

In the wake of the Kennedy assassination, not only the American public but people all over the world were about ready to believe the CIA capable of anything. When Bob Dylan came off his motorcycle in Woodstock, New York, in 1966, conspiracy buffs claimed the CIA had fixed it. On a more rational level, many claimed that the Company had been in cahoots with the FBI in a conspiracy to kill the Rev. Martin Luther King Jr. and had organized the escape to Europe of the assassin/patsy, James Earl Ray. Fingers

SOME KILLINGS THE COMPANY SCARCELY BOTHERED TO CONCEAL

were also pointed when Bobby Kennedy was shot by supposed "lone nut" Sirhan Sirhan. Claims were made that Sirhan was a CIA brainwashed assassin, programmed by Dr. William Bryan Jr. of MKULTRA and "handled" by a mysterious woman in a polka dot dress, and that LAPD officers with ties to the Agency took every pain to conceal any evidence that didn't support the explanation of Sirhan as a lone gunman.

Although the CIA might not actually have put a bullet in Salvador Allende—in fact, the Chilean socialist president was either shot by the military or took his own life—it did totally orchestrate the economic destabilization and military coup that brought him down and put General Augusto Pinochet at the head of the murderous Nazi-style oligarchy that would rule the country for the next 20 years. When exiled Allende supporter Orlando Letelier was blown up in his car in Washington DC by a DINA hit squad (the Chilean secret police), the CIA, under George Bush, did such a casual job of covering up CIA involvement that the story became public within a month. Some killings the Company scarcely bothered to conceal at all. When dictator Rafael Trujillo was killed after 30 years in power in the Dominican Republic, the CIA involvement was almost immediately revealed, but what did it matter? The Dominican strongman had become too corrupt and brutal even for them.

By the 1980s, however, the Company's reputation for indiscriminate murder was causing so many problems that,

left A CIA-backed military coup brings down the elected Chilean government.

below General Augusto Pinochet, Salvador Allende's successor, who would rule Chile for the next two decades.

★
77
=

TOO CORRUPT AND BRUTAL EVEN FOR THEM

below and left
Sheik Fadlallah, the leader of Hezbollah, escaped death in the botched, CIA-ordered, bomb attack. The CIA even added to the misery of civil-war-torn Beirut by mounting their own bomb outrage.

when Ronald Reagan's CIA Director William Casey decided to flex Company muscles in the Middle East by killing Sheik Fadlallah, the head of the Islamic fundamentalist group, Hezbollah, he figured it was maybe not a good idea to have the action in any way traceable to the Agency itself. Instead of using Company "assets," the job was contracted out to a hit team from the Saudi Arabian secret service. Unfortunately, the resulting car bomb attack in Beirut was so badly botched that it not only failed to kill the Sheik, but took out 80 innocent civilians instead. The attack was almost immediately connected to the CIA, the situation in the Middle East markedly worsened, and only Casey's close personal relationship with Ronald Reagan saved his job.

The Vicki Morgan case

While Casey attempted to mix it up with terrorists at the CIA and Oliver North went about his illegal international intrigues in the White House basement, a much more minor

★
=

scandal in 1983 also cast yet another shadow of doubt on the Reagan-era Company. Model and party girl, Vicki Morgan, had been the longtime mistress of Alfred Bloomingdale, the founder of the Diner's Club and heir to the Bloomingdale's department store fortune. Bloomingdale was also a close friend of Ronald Reagan, an unofficial advisor, a member of his personal "kitchen cabinet," and an appointee to the Foreign Intelligence Advisory Board. On July 7th, 1983 Morgan was found beaten to death in her Hollywood apartment. Her roommate, Marvin Pancost, immediately confessed to the slaying. Initially, it seemed to be nothing more than another sordidly pointless Hollywood murder out on the fringes of showbusiness, but then some bizarre rumors began to circulate.

A year earlier, when Bloomingdale had been hospitalized for throat cancer, his wife Betsy had attempted to end his relationship with Morgan by cutting off the money that Bloomingdale had been paying her. Vicki immediately retaliated by threatening to go public with the story of her relationship with Bloomingdale. Apparently it had been more than just a one-on-one romance. Vicki had acted as hostess at regular S&M, whip and bondage parties thrown by Bloomingdale for prominent figures in the Reagan administration, and she had video tapes to prove it. She went to the William Morris Agency with a tell-all book proposal, but this project was supposedly derailed by powerful Hollywood figures looking to protect Reagan's interests. Vicki then threatened to go directly to the media, but died before she could make a public statement. Five days after the murder, attorney Robert Steinberg claimed that he had the Bloomingdale orgy tapes, but was unable to produce them when ordered by a court. They had been mysteriously stolen from his briefcase.

Marvin Pancost was convicted of the murder on the strength of his confession and that should have been the end of the Vicki Morgan story, except that weird tidbits of information continued to surface. Pancost turned out to have a history of confessing to crimes that he never committed, all the way back to when he tried to take the blame for the Manson Family, Tate/LaBianca murders. The LAPD investigation of the Morgan murder was revealed to be a badly botched job. The crime scene had not been sealed for 24 hours, and in the words of author Anne Louis Bardach, "this is really a story of police negligence." These items were more than enough to start the conspiracy mill grinding and fingers were again pointed at the CIA. The most popular interpretation was that someone in the Reagan camp had used Bloomingdale's intelligence connections to enlist Agency help to silence Morgan, before copies of the sex party tapes could find their way to tabloid TV and maybe bring down the supposedly ultra-moral Republican presidency.

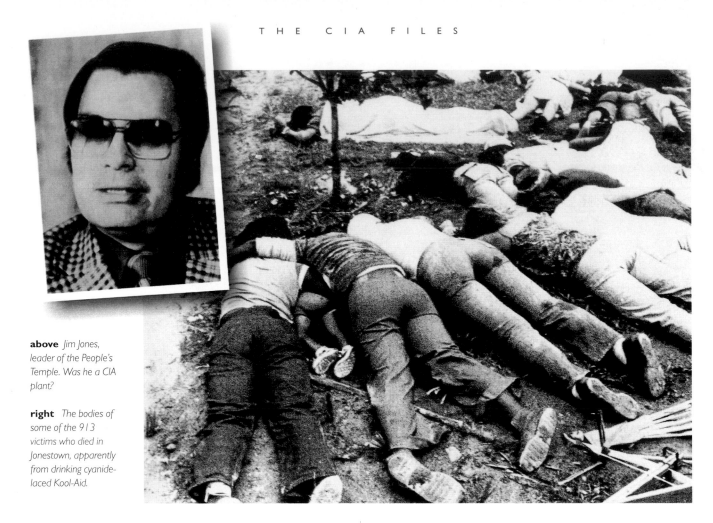

above *Jim Jones, leader of the People's Temple. Was he a CIA plant?*

right *The bodies of some of the 913 victims who died in Jonestown, apparently from drinking cyanide-laced Kool-Aid.*

★
80
=

Jim Jones and the Jonestown massacre

If the Vicki Morgan story seems far-fetched, the connection between the CIA and Jim Jones and the Jonestown massacre in Guyana has to seem stranger than any fiction. The story as generally accepted is as follows: the charismatic preacher Jim Jones founded the People's Temple in Ukiah, California, and subsequently moved to San Francisco, where the People's Temple formed a powerful political/religious coalition of poor whites and blacks and made important connections to the liberal city administration of Mayor George Moscone and Supervisor Harvey Milk. In the mid-1970s, Jones' mental health started to deteriorate and he may have been using amphetamines. He became increasingly paranoid that the CIA were out to get him. In 1977, he moved the entire Temple—with close to 1000 followers—to a jungle plantation in the former British colony of Guyana, where he sought to establish a utopian religious commune.

In Guyana, instead of finding refuge, Jones' paranoia grew worse. Rumors of abuse, beatings, and starvation in the Jonestown commune began to filter back to the USA, and a fact finding group led by Congressman Leo Ryan went to Jonestown to investigate. This visit is accepted as the final factor in pushing Jones over the edge and convincing him that some kind of biblical apocalypse was at hand. Jones' followers machine-gunned Ryan and his party to death as they were leaving Jonestown in two light planes. After these killings, Jones and his followers—some 913 victims in all—committed mass suicide by drinking Kool-Aid laced with cyanide. The story was horrific, to be sure, but essentially nothing more than one more mass freakout by religious extremists, and certainly with no apparent connection to plots by the CIA or any other agency.

As with so many other strange, CIA-related stories, however, facts began to float to the surface that didn't quite fit with the generally accepted line. In the week after the mass suicide, Moscone and Milk were murdered in a seemingly unrelated incident. The Guyanese coroner's report—that received virtually no coverage in the US media—totally contradicted the idea of mass suicide and clearly stated that the majority of victims had either been shot or injected with lethal toxins, and that only two had committed suicide. Far from being afraid of the CIA, Jones was revealed to have maintained a number of solid links with the Company. He had been close personal friends from

THOSE WHO DO NOT REMEMBER THE PAST ARE CONDEMNED TO REPEAT IT.

HE SOUGHT TO ESTABLISH A UTOPIAN RELIGIOUS COMMUNE

boyhood with the notorious Agency torture expert, Dan Mitrione, who had been a CIA advisor to security forces in both Brazil and Uruguay. Jones had been in Brazil at the same time Mitrione was stationed there, and later, in Guyana, he had been in close touch with other agents at the US embassy in Georgetown, and a CIA operative was even supposed to have been present in Jonestown at the time of the massacre. Jones also apparently had ties with an evangelical media group called World Vision that was later revealed to be a CIA front organization (a front organization that is also alleged to have had contact with John Hinckley, who attempted to assassinate Ronald Reagan, and Mark Chapman, who shot John Lennon). On the other side of the coin, Congressman Ryan was an outspoken critic of the CIA and, had he lived, he would have introduced a bill into the House compelling the Agency to clear all covert actions with congressional

oversight committees. The final twist in the tale was that photographs of the body alleged to be that of Jim Jones, failed to show some distinctive tattoos.

Once again, we can only turn to the less than reliable conspiracy mill for any attempt to make sense of all this—and what we get from there is a truly nightmare scenario. According to a number of authors and websites, Jonestown was nothing more than a CIA behavioral experiment—only one in a series of many that are much more adequately documented. The supposed commune in the jungle was, in fact, little short of an experimental concentration camp where "inmates" were observed and tested while being pushed to the limits of physical and psychological stress. That the US government could be connected with anything so monstrous seems beyond belief, except that the equally unbelievable but totally proven reports of other CIA mind-control operations like MKULTRA and MKNAOMI start to make the Jonestown theories all too horribly plausible.

CHAPTER FOUR

THROUGH THE LOOKING GLASS

The Battlefield of the Mind

If the spy game has its very own Holy Grail, it has to be the power of mind control. The ultimate fantasy of any intelligence agency is to employ agents who could always be trusted to remain loyal because they were incapable of doing anything else; agents who could never be turned, or bribed, or otherwise induced to betray their bosses, because their brains were locked down in such a way it made them literally incapable of doing such a thing. Down the years, many things have been tried to achieve this condition of counter-espionage perfection—hypnosis, drugs, fear of torture, intensive psychological training, conditioning for a fanatical loyalty to a country, individual, or ideology. To one degree or another, these things have worked, but no spy net has ever achieved anything close to total perfection or a complete control of its agents.

★

83

Most spymasters have relied heavily on the recruitment of the right kind of agents in the first place. This is why, during World War Two, "Wild Bill" Donovan looked to the Ivy League colleges to find his initial core of OSS operatives. The combination of education, class, and a certain tradition of patriotism in the people is as reliable as could be hoped. Also, in a state of open warfare against the Germans and Japanese, the situation was fairly simplistic.

facing page *The mind games of the 1950s and 1960s (clockwise from top left): Cardinal Josef Mindszenty, who was supposedly brainwashed by the communists; Dr. Sidney Gottlieb, the head of mind control operations for the CIA; Jimi Hendrix, who saw psychedelic drugs as the key to freedom; Joseph Stalin, who slaughtered his way to an empire controlled by fear.*

above *Senator Joe McCarthy, whose communist witch hunting with the House Un-American Activities Committee (HUAC) brought America to the verge of countrywide, reds-under-the-bed, psychosis.*

right *The Soviets parade their missiles in Moscow's Red Square. By the early 1950s, the Cold War had become a potentially deadly nuclear face off.*

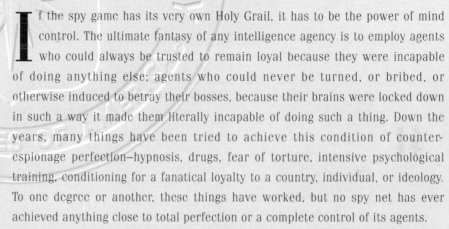

right *During the Korean War, "human wave" assault troops showed such a total disregard for their own deaths that fears grew in the US that they were under some form of mind control.*
below *Stalin; the Red Menace personified.*

The opposing sides were easily definable, without too many gray areas, and the OSS was hardly plagued by traitors, double agents, or defectors. The OSS against the Nazis or the agents of Imperial Japan was a clear-cut case of the good guys against the bad guys. Things radically changed, though, when the CIA took over and the Cold War got underway. Suddenly, the newly formed Agency was functioning in a shadow world that was almost entirely one of gray areas. It found itself doing business with Latin American, would-be dictators, ex-Nazis, and the home-grown Mafia. The idea of having a means of control, a guarantee of loyalty, started to look very attractive.

When Allen Dulles became director of the Agency in 1953, America was already in an advanced state of collective anxiety. The Soviets had the bomb, the Korean War had not gone well, and, at home, the House Un-American Activities Committee (HUAC) under Senator Joe McCarthy was conducting its witchhunt against supposed domestic communists. To America, in those near-psychotic times, the idea of a communist was, almost literally, like something out of the film *Invasion of the Body Snatchers*. They looked like you and me; they talked like you and me; they dróve a car and went to their jobs like you and me; they were indistinguishable from the rest of the population, but, all the time, they were supposedly spreading the disease-like contagion of subversion, the infection that it was imagined could destroy freedom and democracy.

The Korean "human waves"

While McCarthy looked for Reds under American beds, the Company at Langley was also receiving some disquieting reports from behind the Iron Curtain. Allied POWs returning from Korea told stories of being subjected to intensive psychological conditioning, in some cases of sufficient intensity to break certain individuals and cause them to turn on their fellow prisoners and sign spurious confessions of war crimes for the Chinese communists. During the Korean War, the US Army had also encountered the "human wave" tactics of the Chinese and North Koreans, in which massive, saturation infantry attacks overwhelmed allied positions by sheer weight of numbers. The stories were that the front lines of these human waves were so certain to be killed in the first few seconds of the attack that they weren't even issued with rifles.

The Joint Chiefs of Staff wanted to know from the CIA how the communists could instill such fanatical loyalty into their troops that they would willingly charge to their certain deaths in seemingly in-exhaustible numbers. Were they high on drugs? Had they been somehow conditioned beyond the point of fear, or was it the old racist story that Orientals had a "different attitude to death." The kamikaze pilots of World War Two had after all been prepared to make suicide attacks for their emperor, but the Divine Wind had never blown with the intensity of

REPORTS FROM BEHIND THE IRON CURTAIN

these human waves. The theory of Oriental difference was also compounded by the recent memories of Stalin's Moscow purge trials at which political prisoners, tough Russian apparatchiks, had confessed to seemingly impossible crimes. The deep-rooted fear was that the communists had developed a system that could somehow alter the most basic workings of the mind. The term "brainwashing" was being bandied around with increasing frequency.

If any single incident kicked the US fear of a communist mind control into high gear, it was the trial in Hungary in 1949 of Cardinal Josef Mindszenty. The deposed leader of the country's Catholic church showed up in court, glazed and disorientated, and confessed to all manner of treason and crimes against the state that he clearly would not ever have been in a position to commit. After studying films and audio tapes of the Mindszenty trial, the Agency issued a Special Security Memorandum declaring that "some unknown force had been used on the Cardinal" and went on to speculate that the Hungarian secret police had used "either hypnosis or drugs, or a combination of the two."

MKULTRA

The mass paranoia of the early 1950s was, again, nothing short of science fiction, and when Allen Dulles took over the CIA in 1953 he began to look for some science-fiction-like solutions. Even the name of the super-secret new department that was created to develop these solutions was like something out of a low budget sci-fi movie—MKULTRA—although there was absolutely nothing low budget about it. The start-up money for MKULTRA ran to an initial $300,000, perhaps small in comparison to the modern price tag for a cruise missile or a Stealth bomber, but, by the standards of the time, it was a fairly hefty sum, and Dulles assured Ph.D. chemist, Dr. Sidney Gottlieb, the man chosen to head up MKULTRA, that there was plenty more where that came from. This was the point that at least one section of the Company entered a looking glass world where black could easily be white, and nothing was what it seemed.

MKULTRA was the CIA's contribution to the counter-intelligence grail quest. Although it branched out in many

★

85

=

left The suicide attacks of World War Two Japanese kamikaze pilots were a precursor of the "human wave" attacks of the Korean War.
below Cardinal Josef Mindszenty seemed to have either been drugged, brainwashed, or both.

directions, its main objectives were essentially fourfold, and fell under the broad headings of:

1. mind and behavior control;
2. advanced brainwashing and the remolding of minds and belief systems;
3. truth drugs that would make other methods of interrogation obsolete,
4. techniques for psychological warfare on a mass scale.

In many respects, MKULTRA was the offspring of the OSS dirty tricks department that "Wild Bill" Donovan had set up to raise "merry hell" during World War Two, except that, rather than raising "merry hell," MKULTRA at times looked as though its objective might actually be to create a hell right here on Earth, with objectives so fiendishly grandiose that they scared even some hardened insiders.

Experimenting with drugs

From the very start, drugs were a particular preoccupation of MKULTRA. The reasons for this were fairly obvious. On one hand, Gottlieb himself was a chemist, and Helms seemed firmly to believe in the words of Aldous Huxley—author of the novel *Brave New World* and an early LSD researcher—when he declared that drugs might be "the doors of perception." Helms not only urgently wanted the kind of mind-bending truth drugs it was feared the Soviets might be developing, but he may even have contemplated using drugs on a mass scale to create a "brave new world" of his own, although this would have been a very different place from the one imagined by most advocates of psycho-chemical revolution.

THE MKULTRA MASTERMIND

Outwardly, Sidney Gottlieb was the most unlikely figure, among all the Ivy League spy chiefs at the CIA Headquarters at Langley, to head the CIA's advanced mind control program through three decades. He was Jewish, born and raised in the Bronx, educated at Cal Tech, and held a Ph.D. in chemistry. He was a somewhat strange individual with a pronounced stammer and a clubfoot. Despite his physical handicap, his passionate hobby was folk dancing and, when away from the Agency, he lived in a rural cabin outside Washington with his wife and four children, where he raised goats, made his own cheese, and grew Christmas trees for commercial sale. It's rumored that, along with Henry Kissinger and Edward Teller, one of the fathers of the H bomb, Sid Gottlieb was a model for Stanley Kubrick's Dr. Strangelove.

In psychological parlance, Gottlieb was a "compensator," an individual who would go the crucial extra yard just to prove himself. One associate recalled: "when you watched him, you gained more and more respect because he was willing to work

so hard to get an idea across."

Gottlieb had one major advantage at Langley. His patron was the tall, ambitious, patrician Richard Helms, a favorite of Allen Dulles, who would rise to be CIA Director himself during the Vietnam era. Helms liaised directly between Dulles and Gottlieb, totally protecting his protégé from the jealousies and petty bureaucracy that plagued the Company. As a result of this, Sid Gottlieb could do exactly what he wanted, and was free to follow his obsessions and conduct experimental programs that, at times, were nothing short of highly bizarre, with virtually no one but Helms calling him to account. And Helms apparently doted on Gottlieb believing that, one day, he might uncover the secrets of the espionage universe, like some spook world Einstein. This secret, as Helms told a Senate hearing in 1977, was the certainty of total control by any means necessary: "The clandestine operator...is trained that you can't count on the honesty of your agent to do exactly what you want, or report to you accurately,

left *The idea of a totally controlled civilian population had been presented as science fiction as early as 1926 in the Fritz Lang film* Metropolis.

87

THE KEY TO THE COMPLETE CONTROL OF THE HUMAN MIND

Of all the drugs that sparked the interest of MKULTRA, LSD was at the head of the list. For almost 20 years, the Company firmly believed that d-lysergic acid diethylamide 25 (the full chemical name for LSD) could be the key to the complete control of a human mind. The hallucinations and violent mood swings created during the course of an LSD experience seemed to promise what the CIA had always desired—the capacity to erase or alter memory, to change basic principles and though patterns, to "turn" an enemy agent, or to be the ultimate truth serum capable of wringing the deepest secrets from an operative's very soul. More than 15 years before the first hippie strapped on a headband or Jerry Garcia played his first note with the Grateful Dead, the Agency was dropping acid on both willing subjects and unsuspecting citizens. It is possible the dreams of MKULTRA went even further. If used in the correct proportions and with the needed delivery systems, LSD might be the means to bring entire populations under total and continuous thought control. What most people would perceive as the Orwellian nightmare of a docile civilian population, who could be driven like sheep, obeying the orders of their self-appointed Agency masters without hesitation or question, was seen by the Agency as too tempting a vision to ignore.

Another factor in the attraction of LSD was, as one MKULTRA operative put it, "such minute quantities had such a terrific effect." Weight for weight, LSD was a million times more powerful than the hashish that had been around for more than a thousand years, and several thousand times more powerful than mescaline, which had been know to western experimenters since the late 19th century. Enough LSD to affect every man, woman, and child in the United States could easily be packed in a small suitcase. The first research plan was to treat the drug as a potential weapon. "We thought about the possibility of putting some in a city water supply and having the citizens wander around in a more or less happy state, not terribly interested in defending themselves."

The first problem to confront Sid Gottlieb and his researchers at MKULTRA was that, in the early 1950s, almost nothing was known about the effects of LSD. The handbook for most of the groups' initial research was the drug data from the Nazi experiments at Dachau. Unfortunately for Gottlieb, although the Nazis had known about the existence of LSD, they had never used it. The closest that they had come had been to induce hallucinations with the kindred drug mescaline.

DEATHCAMP DRUG FILES

During World War Two, the Germans had developed two crucial drugs—methadone as a substitute for morphine when Nazi opium supplies were cut off, used as a battlefield pain killer, and methadrine, that was used to keep aircrews awake for protracted flight missions and is the godfather of today's street "speed." These and many other drugs had all been tested on prisoners at Dachau; some of the others included heroin, morphine, hashish, Benzedrine, barbiturates—often in conjunction with alcohol—and various nerve gas derivatives similar to what would eventually be known on the street as STP. Victims were regularly overdosed to measure toxicity levels and addictions were created and then withdrawal symptoms studied. The truly scary part of the way that the CIA incorporated much of this material into their early drug research is that they appear to have become infected by some of the Nazi attitudes and methods. When the

existence of MKULTRA and examples of its work were first publicly revealed to the Rockefeller Commission investigating the CIA in the mid-1970s, in the wake of Watergate and the fall of Saigon, the first shock was the cavalier lack of concern on the part of Gottlieb and his people for the human guinea pigs—volunteers or otherwise—who were the subjects of their bizarre experiments.

Most of the available data could only come from the drug's inventor, Dr. Albert Hoffman. Some ten years earlier, while developing the drug for the Sandoz pharmaceutical empire in their labs on the outskirts of Basel, Switzerland, he had accidentally ingested a tiny quantity – less than one hundred thousandth of an ounce—and found himself precipitated into a hallucinatory dream world for a period of almost 12 hours.

Before MKULTRA could even think about dosing entire populations, they had to conduct a large number of individual tests on a representative sampling of subjects. At first, with the same wild cowboy abandon of the old OSS, the MKULTRA boys tried the drug on themselves and their colleagues. This kind of do-it-yourself investigation, however, proved to be too disorganized and haphazard. About all it demonstrated was that LSD had different effects on different people. Richard Helms, as the go-between linking Gottlieb and Director Dulles, also didn't

take very kindly to the idea that operatives of one of the Agency's most highly secret research operations were spending a good deal of their working lives tripped out of their minds!

The first serious LSD experiments were conducted along what would become traditional CIA covert lines. Using dummy charitable foundations, large sums of money, in the form of grants and endowments, were channeled to selected hospitals around the USA on the understanding that they would be used to run LSD tests, primarily on mental patients and student volunteers, under the guise of academic medical research. Among the hospitals included in the program—completely unaware of the primary source of the funds—were Boston Psychopathic, Mt. Sinai and Columbia University in New York, and the University of Illinois Medical School. Although the hospital tests were of considerable value, by their very nature they had to be kept within certain bounds.

Free drugs for prisoners

No such limits had to be observed at the National Addiction Research Center (NARC), which was part of the huge drug hospital attached to the Federal Penitentiary in Lexington, Kentucky. With a literally captive population, LSD could be crash tested beyond any reasonable limits. Word was circulated through the prison grapevine that incarcerated addicts would be rewarded with supplies of the narcotic of their choice if they volunteered. The deal was a simple one: take a hit of acid and be rewarded with a shot of heroin or cocaine. Many addicts didn't give it a second thought. The drugs used as rewards in the NARC experiments were reputed to be of the highest quality and purity, far above anything the cons could hope to score on the street.

Unfortunately for the inmate volunteers, the tests didn't stop with just one hit of acid. Dr.

LSD COULD BE CRASH TESTED BEYOND ANY REASONABLE LIMITS

Harris Isbell quickly gave in to CIA pressure to start testing the outer limits of endurance to the drug. In one test, he kept seven men continuously tripping for 77 straight days. Today, such prolonged highs are virtually unthinkable. In the hippie culture of the 1960s, the common belief was that no one could stay continuously high for more than three or four days, at the most perhaps a full week, without sustaining permanent psychological damage. Dr. Hunter S. Thompson, who has made a career out of writing about his prodigious, self-inflicted drug and alcohol excesses, noted that, after only three straight days on acid, he felt "his brain boiling away in the sun" and his other faculties "reduced to their reptilian antecedents." The effect of 77 days, therefore, is totally unimaginable.

Drugs and sex

If strange things were happening in Lexington, even stranger events were about to take place in the city of San Francisco, where a one-time Federal narcotics agent called George White, now doing contract work for Sid Gottlieb, was setting up a string of clandestine "safe houses" where CIA-hired local prostitutes would slip the drug to their unsuspecting clients while the boys from MKULTRA

left *Some of the first human guinea pigs in CIA drug experiments were the inmates of Federal prisons.*

THE SUB-WORLD OF PIMPS AND HOOKERS, JUNKIES AND PUSHERS

above *During the 1960s, an aerosol-based drug delivery system was allegedly tested in the New York subway system.*
left *Singer Billie Holliday was one of the victims of George White, a narcotics officer with a taste for busting celebrities.*

watched and filmed from behind false walls and one-way mirrors. The hiring of George White was a perfect example of how MKULTRA seemed able to push any limit if the goal was worth it. White was a flamboyant, hard drinking character from some kind of Mickey Spillane tradition, who more than once shot holes in a hotel room ceiling while armed and blind drunk. Built like the proverbial brick outhouse and with a bullet-like shaved head, he had served with the OSS during the war and then returned to the BNDD (the Bureau of Narcotics and Dangerous Drugs—the forerunner of the DEA), working for Harry Anslinger, the man who single-handedly started the War on Drugs. It seems relatively certain that, while working as a narc (narcotics agent), he set up the singer Billie Holliday on a drug bust. Definitely, a jury refused to give credit to the evidence he presented.

Blocked once from joining the CIA as being too much of rough diamond for the Ivy League Company, White only joined MKULTRA because Gottlieb wanted him, and Gottlieb—through Helms—invariably got what he wanted. In the wake of George White, the CIA would recruit many more socially unacceptable mavericks, whom they could maintain at arm's length to do their dirty work. And make no mistake, White was in it for the dirty work. Gottlieb had been drawn to him because of his intimate knowledge of the street, the sub-world of pimps and hookers, junkies and pushers, the basic consumer/distributor low-life nuts and bolts of the drug culture. Like the cons in Lexington, a

hapless dope fiend from the streets, inadvertently caught up in the CIA's nightmare of drug tests, was unlikely to spill the beans, and if he did, who would believe him or her?

The CIA's Summer of Love

This use of people with limited credibility could possibly have given rise to what may have been the CIA's most ambitious drug experiment. The concept of a mass test of LSD on a center of population had constantly resurfaced on the MKULTRA wish list since the days when they fantasized about putting acid in a city's water supply, or later, supposedly dry-tested an aerosol-style delivery system for hallucinogenic chemicals like LSD in the New York subway system. At this point, we descend once again into the sub-basement of paranoia and conspiracy theory, but certain parts of an incomplete jigsaw at least tend to suggest that Sid Gottlieb, presumably through George White, may have

actually decided to facilitate the release of large quantities of LSD, packaged as a street drug, into the bohemian enclaves of San Francisco's Haight-Ashbury and North Beach. If this was truly the case, it would have meant that the CIA was directly responsible for creating the Summer of Love, hippies, the psychedelic counter-culture, and all that followed. The line from Sid Gottlieb to Jimi Hendrix might seem an implausibly convoluted thread, but is one that might just exist.

The documented facts and the most recurrent rumors are pretty much as follows:

- George White was both highly connected and deeply enmeshed in the San Francisco drug culture; he knew the cops, the informers, the addicts, and the dealers. He certainly had all the resources to introduce a brand new drug onto the street.

- In 1959, MKULTRA was operating out of the Veterans' Hospital in Menlo Park, San Francisco, offering, at that early stage, $100 to any subject who would take LSD and allow his or her responses to be observed and recorded.

- One of these volunteers at Menlo Park was author Ken Kesey, best known for the book and film *One Flew over the Cuckoo's Nest.* Kesey managed to walk out of the hospital with some samples of LSD, which he used to turn on himself and friends, including beat generation icon Neal Cassady. Two years later, Kesey would take an entire psychedelic roadshow across the country in the form of the Merry Pranksters and their legendary bus, dropping acid on everyone from Timothy Leary to the Hells Angels.

- Poet Allen Ginsberg took his first LSD as part of a CIA-sponsored clinical study. (He recalled the experience was "like being hooked into the brain of Big Brother.") The psilocybin Timothy Leary used for his early experiments at Harvard may also have come indirectly from MKULTRA as part of one of their covert programs.

above *Poet Allen Ginsberg took his first LSD as part of a CIA-sponsored study. From that point on, he saw the drug as means of mind expansion and self realization that should not be controlled by the government.*

★
92
=

• The acid used by the Merry Pranksters, and the acid that was reputed to be the best on the street, was created by a renegade, counter-culture chemist and near genius, Augustus Owsley Stanley III, whose production line, at its psychedelic peak, was turning out tabs of LSD in batches of one and half million a time.

The missing link—the actual smoking gun—in all this is of course the crucial connection between Owsley and MKULTRA. That a George White contact or another of Gottlieb's people had given Owsley any aid in setting up his manufacturing process or, indeed, that Owsley may have played the Company for his own ends and won, has often been postulated, but never proved. Few smoking guns ever remain in the CIA files. Despite its excesses, the Company has always been more careful than that. All we are left with is the intriguing, but infinitely possible, suggestion, that MKULTRA, at the apex of its power, may have actually attempted to trip out an entire city in the country it was supposed to be protecting from exactly that kind of thing!

If the acid that fueled the Summer of Love did come indirectly from the CIA, it would certainly have contributed to the eventual decision that LSD, although useful in certain circumstances, especially to create disorientation and fear, was too unpredictable in its effects to be the key to mind control.

THE PSYCHEDELIC VICTIM

Whatever else may have happened while **MKULTRA** were conducting their experiments on the human mind, at least one well-documented fatality occurred. Dr. Frank Olson was a civilian chemist working at the Army Chemical Corps' Special Operations Division (SOD) at Fort Detrick, Maryland, around the time that Sid Gottlieb and **MKULTRA** started their LSD testing. Although SOD and the **CIA** were not directly linked, there was a considerable liaison between the two organizations and Olson, because his special field of study was the airborne delivery of bacterial weapons, had worked particularly closely with Gottlieb and others in **MKULTRA**. So closely in fact, that the relationship would ultimately kill him.

Although after Olson's death, Sid Gottlieb would attempt to minimize his role in the tragedy by claiming that he had "spoken in general terms to Olson and other SOD scientists about the possibility of their, at some point, taking the drug LSD," it seems absolutely certain that Gottlieb had personally spiked Frank Olson with a major dose of acid during a three-day annual retreat at a hunting lodge in the woods of rural Maryland. These retreats were designed so the specialists from the army and the **CIA** could get together and compare notes.

What Frank Olson didn't know was that he was going to be the unwitting guinea pig for a demonstration of Sid Gottlieb's new chemical toy. It is virtually certain that the drug was slipped to Olson on the second night of the retreat in an after-dinner liqueur, almost like a schoolboy prank. For the next eight hours, unaware that he'd been drugged, Olson suffered mindwrenching hallucinations that he could only explain to himself as the onset of some kind of sudden and violent mental breakdown.

In the days and weeks after the incident, Olson became increasingly depressed to the point that he was unable to deal with his wife and children with whom he had a previously close and loving relationship. Gottlieb and Olson's boss at SOD, Lt. Colonel Vincent Ruwet, decided that Olson needed medical help. However, instead of taking Olson to a psychiatrist, he was delivered into the care of Dr. Harold Abramson, a New York immunologist—not because Abramson was the best man for the job, but because he had top secret CIA clearance. Under Abramson's care, Olson's state of mind continued to deteriorate. He increasingly felt that "the CIA was out to get him." (Not all that unreasonable under the circumstances.) Abramson declared himself unable to cope.

Olson agreed to let himself be taken by Gottlieb's deputy, Robert Lashbrook, from New York to Chestnut Lodge—a sanitarium in Rockville, Maryland, with CIA-cleared psychiatrists on the staff. Unfortunately, Lashbrook and Olson had to wait a day for plane reservations, and the highly disturbed patient and his MKULTRA minder had to spend the night in the Statler Hotel. In the early hours of the morning, Lashbrook woke, just in time to see Olson go out through the glass of the hotel room window at a dead run. Their room was on the tenth floor, and Olson was history the moment he hit the ground.

The truth finally comes out

Needless to say, all hell broke loose, and the cover-up started even as the crowd was gathering around the body on the street below, and would remain in place for the next two decades until the matter was opened up by the Rockefeller Commission. The CIA secretly admitted that Olson's suicide may have been "triggered" by the LSD, but it was never made known outside the Agency, even to Olson's surviving family.

For 20 years, Alice Olson and her three children believed that their husband and father had died as a result of a massive psychological breakdown. Even when the case was cited by the Rockefeller Commission, Frank Olson was not personally identified, reference only being made to an unnamed SOD employee. Alice Olson, however, recognized the case as being that of her husband and sued the government. In 1975, President Gerald Ford apologized to the Olson family and Congress passed a bill to pay them $750,000 in compensation. The suit thus never came to court. It had also been suggested that Sid Gottlieb should be in some way reprimanded after the incident, but Allen Dulles quashed this on the grounds that it would hinder "the spirit of initiative and enthusiasm so necessary in our work."

HE WOKE JUST IN TIME TO SEE OLSON GO OUT THROUGH THE GLASS OF THE HOTEL ROOM WINDOW AT A DEAD RUN

You must not miss the first five minutes to know what it's all about!

Frank Sinatra

when you've seen it all, you'll swear there's never been anything like it!

Laurence Harvey

Janet Leigh

The Manchurian Candidate 'A'

Angela Lansbury · Henry Silva · James Gregory

Produced by GEORGE AXELROD and JOHN FRANKENHEIMER

Directed by JOHN FRANKENHEIMER Screenplay by GEORGE AXELROD Based upon a Novel by RICHARD CONDON Executive Producer HOWARD W. KOCH An M. C. PRODUCTION

left Director John Frankenheimer's 1962 movie The Manchurian Candidate presented the first fictional portrayal of a brainwashed assassin.

In search of the mindless assassin

The other great mystery, and also the other great goal of MKULTRA, was, of course, the creation of what was known as a Manchurian Candidate. The name came from Richard Condon's novel *The Manchurian Candidate*, later a movie starring Frank Sinatra and Laurence Harvey. The character in the story was an American officer who had been brainwashed by the Chinese communists to unknowingly assassinate a presidential candidate when exposed to a particular stimulus. The fictional idea was wholly based in the fear that the communists had some kind of mind-control system. Subsequently it would emerge that communists, in fact, had no such thing. The effects that had been seen at the show trial of Cardinal Mindszenty and other dissidents were a result of nothing more than extreme brutality, sleep deprivation, long periods of cold and darkness, and long agonizing sessions of relentless questioning. Neither drugs nor hypnosis turned out to have played any major part in so-called communist brainwashing. This revelation, however, didn't halt the CIA in their quest for the agent under complete control, the automaton who would carry out any order and kill if need be, without independent thought and perhaps without subsequent memory of the event. *The Manchurian Candidate* came out as a movie little more than a year before the

THE AUTOMATON WHO WOULD CARRY OUT ANY ORDER

assassination of President Kennedy, and the two became irrevocably linked to both the public mind and that of the CIA. Indeed, the juxtaposition of the two events so disturbed Frank Sinatra, who not only starred in the film but was also one of its producers, that he had it withdrawn from circulation for over 30 years, so worried was he that life might have somehow imitated art, and that the film had provided a possible motivation for Lee Harvey Oswald.

How close the MKULTRA researchers actually came to creating the fully conditioned, mindless assassin is yet another of the CIA secrets that has never been—and probably never will be—made public. Officially, the implication has always been that it was never attempted in the first place or, if it was, the experiment failed. One MKULTRA veteran maintains that Sid Gottlieb and his people knew from the start that, even if a Manchurian Candidate could be hypnotically or chemically programmed, the subject would be unable to function under field conditions. "If you have 100 per cent control, you have 100 per cent dependency. If something happens that you haven't got programmed in, you've got a problem. If you put in flexibility, you lose control."

The hypnosis program

On the other hand, stories persist that a number of near-automaton killers may well have been created, and that some near misses also had to be quickly and quietly covered up. One of the keys to possible attempts selectively to brainwash an assassin was provided by a statement of CIA Director James Angleton, in 1960, when he headed the Company's Counter Intelligence Division. He wrote in a report that a hypnosis program, seemingly a collaboration of Counter Intelligence and MKULTRA, could provide a "potential breakthrough in clandestine technology." Angleton went on to detail how the responsibility for the program would be divided between MKULTRA, whose people would provide the basic research, and Counter Intelligence, who would conduct the "field testing" when the time came.

right *The behavior of defendants at Stalin's show trials of political dissidents convinced future CIA Director James Jesus Angleton (inset) that hypnotism had been used on them and that hypnotic control, if perfected, could be a potent weapon in the Cold War.*

The hypnosis program had three goals. The first was to "induce hypnosis very rapidly in unwitting subjects." The second was to "create durable amnesia," and the third was to "implant an operationally useful post-hypnotic suggestion." Taken in combination, the three goals were the essential building blocks of a Manchurian Candidate. After this opening declaration of intent, the paper trail abruptly terminates. The CIA has neither released nor acknowledged any information on any research or field testing that took place in the next three years. All that has been made public is a heavily censored report of what seems to have been a botched attempt at instant hypnosis some three and a half years later. That two individuals as determined as Angleton and Gottlieb should have gone as far as to make a declaration of intent, and then done nothing about it for three whole years, seems scarcely plausible. The most obvious inference had to be that they actually did produce the automaton assassin, or that the experiment, due to some unforeseen factor, went seriously awry and had to be quickly and effectively buried.

A clue to what might have happened may be provided by the same unnamed MKULTRA veteran who laid out the impracticalities of a so called Manchurian Candidate. This source did concede that, although a hypnotically programmed assassin was of dubious advantage, the same techniques could be used to create a highly effective "patsy," an individual who could be hypnotically conditioned to take the fall for a real killer, and enable an assassin to make an anonymous escape. A hypnotist could "walk" the patsy through a seemingly unrelated series of events, a visit to a store, a conversation with a mailman, a fight at a political rally. The subject would remember everything that happened to him, except that the hypnotist had faked these events. The purpose of the exercise would be to convince the authorities that the patsy had committed a particular crime. Prior to the crime, all of the patsy's actions would appear quite harmless, but, when taken in combined sequence after the event, they would look like clear circumstantial evidence of guilt.

The only seeming weakness of this technique was that the subject's post-hypnotic amnesia might not hold up under police interrogation. Even that, though, might be turned to an advantage. If the patsy already had a record of

paranoia or instability, who would believe him when he claimed he'd been hypnotised by agents of the Central Intelligence Agency? And, of course, if he just happened to be shot either while resisting arrest or in police custody...

The Oswald cover-up?

And here we may have the real reason why the records of the Angleton/Gottlieb adventures in hypnosis may have been so effectively buried. Hypnosis consultant Milton Kline categorically states that a Manchurian candidate assassin could be created using the right subject. It would take about six months of intense conditioning, and be subject to all the drawbacks already mentioned. "To build a patsy would take only half that time." And if any individual

in recent history conformed to the exact profile of the created patsy, it had to be Lee Harvey Oswald. In Chapter 3 we already looked at the possibility that Oswald was programmed either by the CIA itself or some renegade group within the Company. If it had been revealed that, at exactly the time of the Kennedy assassination, the Agency was messing around with murder and hypnosis, it would have prompted even more questions regarding Oswald and created even more doubts about the Warren Report than there already were. Hadn't Oswald said it himself during his brief moments with the media in Dallas Police Headquarters? "I'm just a patsy."

Another reason that the quest for a Manchurian Candidate may also have been dropped was that, if the Company put its mind to it, a supply of killers and operatives willing to engage in mayhem and desperate deeds was more than readily available. A few good assassins were not difficult to find. The idea of conditioning men to kill was hardly anything new. Since the Roman Legions, soldiers had been methodically and progressively trained to lose their individuality, to identify with the group, put their fear aside, and to kill as a matter of routine. Marine Corps basic training does exactly that, and, in the case of crack outfits like the US Army Green Berets,

Navy SEALS, and the British SAS, the basics are fine tuned to the point where to kill quickly, with ease and without question, became both a reason for being and a way of life. In a world where Special Service LURPS—long range patrol squads—who had been too long in the bush in Vietnam began collecting the ears of dead Viet Cong, hypnotized hitmen hardly seemed necessary. Also, at the same time as Angleton and Gottlieb were trying to build the perfect assassin, other sections of the Company were making connections with a ready-made group of highly efficient killers who even had their own form of amnesia if picked up by the authorities. This was organized crime— the so-called Mafia—and the CIA was increasingly starting to look on them as a resource to be used when needed. Author and Agency expert Robert Sam Anson wrote of this relationship between the Company and the Mob: "It was

inevitable: Gentlemen wishing to be killers gravitated to killers wishing to be gentlemen."

LSD and hypnotism may have proved to be less than the super spy weapons they were hoped to be, but this didn't stop Sid Gottlieb and those who came after him leaving no stone unturned in their quest for total control of individuals or even societies. In the strange, looking glass world of the CIA, nothing was what it appeared to be and almost nothing was too bizarre or unthinkable not to be worthy of investigation as a potential weapon.

The use of front organizations

Although MKULTRA was officially broken up in 1963, in the wake of the Kennedy assassination, in the land beyond the looking glass only the name was changed. If anything, the

WOODY HARRELSON'S DAD

It was possible that no would have ever noticed Charles Voyd Harrelson if his son Woody had not been the star of TV's *Cheers* and movies like *White Men Can't Jump*, *Natural Born Killers*, and *The People vs Larry Flynt*. Charles Harrelson, a self-confessed organized crime hit man, is currently doing life in the Marion Federal Penitentiary in Marion, Illinois, for the 1979 contract murder of U.S. District Judge John H. Wood Jr. In a bizarre incident in the late 1960s, however, Harrelson made the claim that he was one of the killers of JFK—that he had been a marksman, working for a group within the CIA, shooting from the grassy knoll in Dallas's Dealey Plaza. The only problem was that this confession was made by Harrelson, high on cocaine, with a .44 magnum pressed to his own head, and it came at the climax of a six hour standoff with police. The incident had begun when Harrelson had decided that the Corvette he was driving was making too much noise and he had shot it full of holes on the open highway. His statement might have been dismissed had Harrelson not greatly resembled the photographs taken of the "three tramps" arrested in rail yards next to Dealey Plaza immediately after the Kennedy shooting who are believed, by some

assassination theorists, including columnist Jack Anderson, to have been the supposed gunmen on the grassy knoll.

Later Harrelson would deny he had any hand in the Kennedy killing, telling British film maker Nigel Turner: "On November 22nd, 1963, at 12.30, I was having lunch with a friend in a restaurant in Houston, Texas." Evidence does exist, however, that Harrelson did have provable CIA connections and might possibly have been a subject in one or more of MKULTRA's Manchurian Candidate experiments. In an interview with Barbara Walters following the 1997 Academy Awards Show, Woody Harrelson denied that his father was a part of any Kennedy conspiracy, but confirmed that he was a professional hitman, and volunteered the information that Harrelson Sr. had been trained to kill by the CIA. "They created him."

later MKULTRA work went deeper underground, relying increasingly on front organizations, such as the Human Ecology Society. With no visible ties to the Company, the HES channeled funds into colleges, hospitals, and commercial medical research organizations, many of whom didn't have a clue that they were ultimately working for the CIA.

Although the names may have changed, many of the same people would also remain. Sid Gottlieb, under the sponsorship of Richard Helms, would oversee all of the Agency's mind control and related operations until Helms himself was, following the Watergate break in, purged by President Richard Nixon. We may never know the full extent of what MKULTRA and its successors were up to at the furthest extremes. After Nixon fired Helms, Helms and Sid Gottlieb seemed to have gone on a massive shred and burn rampage, destroying a large portion of the most detailed records of the various experimental programs. All we have left is the tips of the various sinister icebergs, and we can only make a semi-informed guess as to what really lay beneath the surface.

We do know that the Human Ecology Society took a

★

98

=

(NOT FOR USE WITHIN 60 MILES OF NEW YORK CITY)
NXP2138928(NS)-3/31/84-NEW YORK: Reputed mob kingpin Paul Castellano(L) is escorted by an FBI agent here 3/30 after he was indicted. Castellano, the alleged head of the Gambino organized-crime family, was charged, along with 20 other people, in a 51-count Federal indictment accusing them of operating a group that committed 25 murders and scores of other crimes. UPI sp/NY NEWS

An obvious alternative to the mind controlled robot killer was for the CIA to simply hire contract killers via mob bosses like Big Paul Castellano (left) or Anthony "Fat Tony" Salerno (above).

THE TIPS OF VARIOUS SINISTER ICEBERGS

particular interest in stress, both in individuals and various sized groups of human beings, but the way it and other front organizations operated made its work even harder to trace than that of the much more centralized MKULTRA. We do know that it conducted experiments in interrogation techniques and possible truth serums on criminal sexual psychopaths at the Ionia State Hospital in Michigan. We also know that a particular interest was taken in social dynamics as they might apply to the destabilization of "unfriendly" countries.

One of the murkiest areas of this kind of was that of electronic brain implants. The general organization that replaced MKULTRA as the main coordinating body was the CIA Office of Research and Development (ORD). ORD, in its turn, used another front foundation, the Scientific Engineering Institute, with Dr. Edwin Land, the inventor of the Polaroid process, as a nominal figurehead, but with Dr. Stephen Aldrich, Sid Gottlieb's successor, really in charge, to set up a 100 acre farm outside of Boston where implant experiments were conducted on dogs, cats, monkeys, and—it has to be presumed—human subjects. One document that was pried loose under the Freedom of Information Act notes that the project was near a "production capability" in brain stimulation, and goes on: "the feasibility of remote control of activities of several species of animals has been demonstrated....Special investigations and evaluations will be conducted towards the applications of these techniques to man." Again, though, the final results have been successfully buried, but, at the very least, they do put a whole new perspective on the homeless crazy on the street who claims that the CIA is sending messages to his brain. Perhaps he isn't as crazy as we assume, but just a failed experiment turned lose by MKULTRA and ORD to babble and wander.

One of the more fiendish aspects of these indirectly funded and fronted research programs is that many of the scientists employed by them not only didn't know that they were working for the CIA, but also believed that they were doing work to relieve human suffering rather than exploring methods to create it. A specialist in brain chemistry might be told that he or she might be pursuing a line of investigation related to—say—migraine headaches and assumed that the data would be used to contribute to a cure, when its real use was to see if pain spasms could be induced in human subjects.

Not all the post-MKULTRA research was quite so demonic. J.C. King, the Company's former head of the Western Hemisphere Division, who was fired after the Bay of Pigs fiasco, found a lucrative retirement occupation. With a CIA front organization called the Amazon Natural Drug Company picking up the tab, King was able to float down jungle rivers in a luxuriously appointed houseboat, "with a glass of scotch at his elbow," searching the backwaters of South America for plants and shamanistic practices that might be of interest to the Agency.

By the end of the 1970s, the CIA had its research net spread so wide that virtually no level of weirdness seemed to be unworthy of its investigation. Although subsequent CIA directors have attempted to give the impression that behavioral, mind control, and drug research had ended with the break up of MKULTRA, author John Marks has more than disproved that. Filing a request under the Freedom of Information Act, Marks demanded all files dated after 1977 on "behavioral research, including but not limited to any research or operation activities related to bio-electric, electric or radio stimulation of the brain,

left Dr. Edwin Land, the inventor of the Polaroid camera, was one prominent figure recruited by the CIA as a legitimizing figurehead for front organizations conducting mind control research for the Company.

electronic destruction of memory, stereotaxic surgery, psychosurgery, hypnotism, parapsychology, radiation, microwaves, and ultrasonics." The CIA responded six months later that ORD had "identified 130 boxes"—a staggering 130 cubic feet of paperwork—that were "reasonably expected to contain behavioral research documents."

Unnamed CIA sources also confirm that, during the 1970s and the 1980s, ORD had, if anything, been going further, faster than even MKULTRA in its unfettered prime under Richard Helms. "We looked into the manipulation of genes...the building of a super soldier like the kamikaze pilot. Creating a subservient society was not out of sight." Another source, once with the Scientific Engineering Institute, describes the work of a colleague who bombarded bacteria with ultraviolet radiation to create deviant germ strains, and how ORD also authorized work in parapsychology." Agency officials wanted to know whether

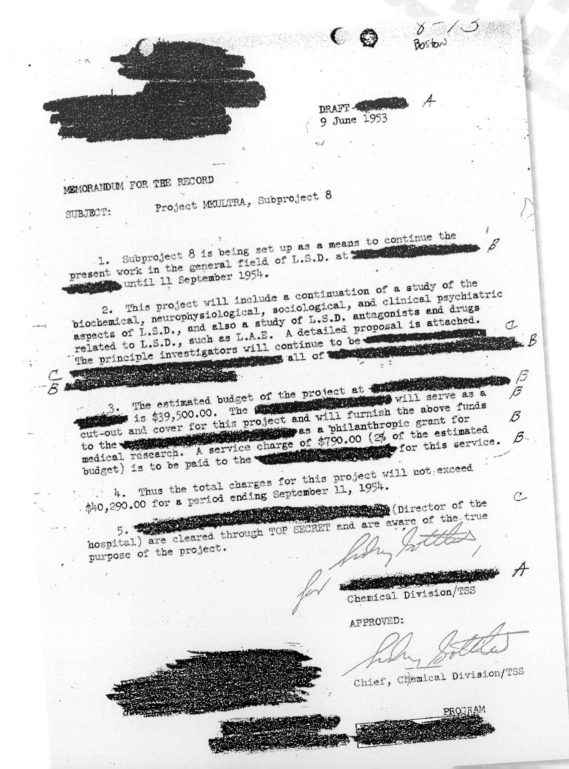

DRAFT A
9 June 1953

MEMORANDUM FOR THE RECORD

SUBJECT: Project MKULTRA, Subproject 8

1. Subproject 8 is being set up as a means to continue the present work in the general field of L.S.D. at ▮▮▮▮▮▮▮▮▮ until 11 September 1954.

2. This project will include a continuation of a study of the biochemical, neurophysiological, sociological, and clinical psychiatric aspects of L.S.D., and also a study of L.S.D. antagonists and drugs related to L.S.D., such as L.A.E. A detailed proposal is attached. The principle investigators will continue to be ▮▮▮▮▮▮▮▮▮ all of ▮▮▮▮▮▮▮▮▮

3. The estimated budget of the project at ▮▮▮▮▮▮ is $39,500.00. The ▮▮▮▮▮▮▮▮ will serve as a cut-out and cover for this project and will furnish the above funds to the ▮▮▮▮▮▮ as a philanthropic grant for medical research. A service charge of $790.00 (2% of the estimated budget) is to be paid to the ▮▮▮▮▮▮ for this service.

4. Thus the total charges for this project will not exceed $40,290.00 for a period ending September 11, 1954.

5. ▮▮▮▮▮▮▮▮ (Director of the hospital) are cleared through TOP SECRET and are aware of the true purpose of the project.

Chemical Division/TSS

APPROVED:

Chief, Chemical Division/TSS

PROGRAM

left *Although the CIA repeatedly tried to downplay or deny its drug experiments, the documentary evidence is hard to refute.*

★
100
=

ALTERED STATES

In the 1980 Ken Russell film *Altered States*, William Hurt played a Boston anthropologist who conducts experiments on himself using psychedelic drugs and a sensory deprivation chamber in which he lays blindfold in a tank of body temperature water listening to white noise over stereo headphones. Under these circumstances, Hurt's character reverts to a primal, almost Neanderthal state. The CIA managed to predate the film by a full 25 years.

In experiments conducted as early as 1955 by Dr. Maitland Baldwin at the National Institute for Health, but with Agency funding and under Agency control, subjects were given various drugs and placed in a similar chamber, dubbed "the Box." Although none of Baldwin's subjects ever reverted to cavemen, the program did have to be suspended when a freaked out soldier volunteer kicked his way out of "the Box."

Other movies have speculated in fictional terms about the use by various intelligence agencies of fanciful forms of mind control. In the 1963 film *The Mindbenders*, sensory deprivation is used on Dirk Bogarde to force him to kill his wife. Two years later, in

The Ipcress File, Michael Caine is all but driven nuts by white noise and a psychedelic lightshow. In 1974, in *The Parallax View*, Warren Beatty is reprogrammed to be an Oswald-style assassin. Although all these may have seemed overly extreme when they were first screened, if the truth were known, they may well have lagged a long way behind reality.

ENEMY PSYCHICS COULD BURN OUT THE BRAINS OF AN ENEMY

psychics could read minds or control them from afar (telepathy). If they could gain information about distant places or people (clairvoyance or remote viewing), if they could predict the future (precognition), or influence the movement of physical objects or even the human mind (photokinesis). The last could be incredibly destructive. Switches to launch nuclear missiles would have to only be moved a few inches. Enemy psychics, with minds honed to laser sharpness, could burn out the brains of an enemy."

Maybe one of the great mercies of the 20th century is that it would seem that the efforts of CIA researchers like Sid Gottlieb and Stephen Aldrich never quite came together as they fully hoped. San Francisco recovered from its purple haze of LSD, Fidel Castro appears to be living to a ripe old age, we the people have not been reduced to programmable zombies, and it has yet to be fully proved that either a programmed hitman or brainwashed patsy was employed in the Kennedy assassination. That is not to say that the looking glass warriors in the CIA may not yet get lucky. The game is far from over and sections of the CIA would still appear to operate in a world that looks on everything from torture to the supernatural as facets of its stock in trade.

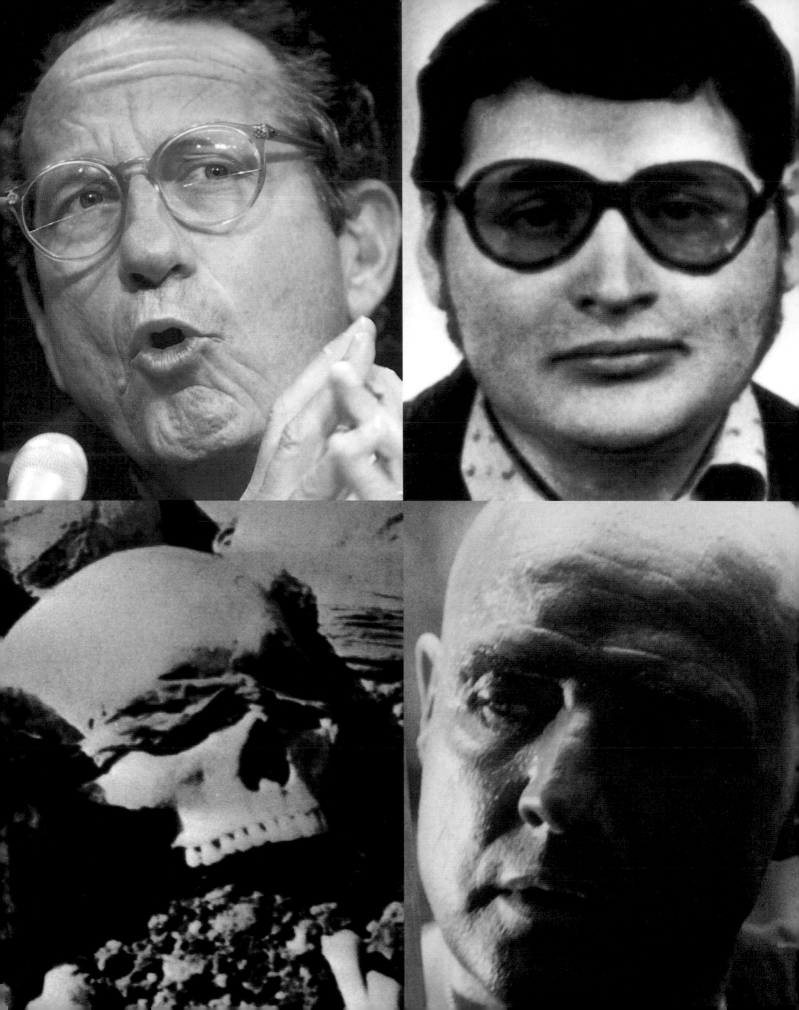

THE HEART OF DARKNESS

Thinking the Unthinkable

"If you look at it for a moment from their point of view, you have to admit that it makes a certain twisted kind of sense. Already in Rio Janeiro, you have kids growing up on the garbage dumps where permanent fires are constantly burning underground, belching toxic smoke full of PCBs and other lethal rubbish. These kids are so brain-damaged from pollution and malnutrition that they are virtually subhuman, IQs of maybe 75 or 89, at the most. At least, that's how the story goes. And on weekends, off-duty police officers go out late at night and hunt and kill them, using death squad techniques that almost certainly were developed at the School of the Americas or the International Police Academy. You can see why they could think 99 per cent of the human race might be a whole lot better off under some kind of microwave broadcast control that keeps that keeps them happy, stupid, and docile. And if you don't think that's possible, I'm telling you, you very seriously need to think again."

"John," who refused to allow us to use his real name because he fears Company reprisals, claims to have been working on the fringes of the CIA and other government agencies for the past 15 years, although he may not be most reliable of informants. It's very easy to dismiss him as one of those guys you

★

103

above *From psyops to psychic spying.*

facing page *The horror, the horror, (clockwise from top left): John Deutch who ran the CIA for Bill Clinton and denied the company was dealing crack; psychics were used in the hunt for Carlos the Jackal; Marlon Brando played the fictional Col. Kurtz; and in Cambodia the horror became real on Pol Pot's killing fields.*

right *Chairman Mao's China; one attempt at a psycho-civilized society?*

meet in New York or Hollywood trying to hustle a living as a professional paranoid. The only part that gives one a moment of pause is that, all too regularly for comfort, some of the things he tells you are then confirmed by some other and seemingly more authoritative source.

Writing for the website "Parascope," English researcher David G. Guyatt notes that the CIA and other government agencies currently possess "innovative technological weapons that do not necessarily kill, but could render disenfranchised segments of society physically inactive, emotionally stupefied, and incapable of meaningful thought."

The goal of total control

What concerns both "John" and David Guyatt is the concept that has become known in intelligence circles as a "psycho-civilized society." The idea of the psycho-civilized society has been around certainly since the establishment of MKULTRA, in 1953, when Sid Gottlieb toyed with the concept of subduing entire populations by the use of drugs, mass hypnosis, or other means. It even has frightening echoes of both Stalin's and Hitler's idea of the New Man, the individual who, via cradle-to-grave propaganda, conditioning, and thought control, could be deprived of all individualism and free will, and whose loyalty to the state and its leaders would be automatic, unquestioning, and permanent. Although the term hadn't been coined at the time, George Orwell speculated on exactly that in his novel *1984*. Mao Tse Tung may have attempted something of the kind when he let loose the Red Guard during China's Cultural Revolution of the mid-1960s, and it was certainly what Pol Pot and Khmer Rouge tried in the next decade by

the mass slaughter on the killing fields of Cambodia, as they worked to destroy all vestiges of previous society in their horrific Year Zero programs.

In some respects, fantasies of this kind should be expected in an environment like that of the CIA, where the ultimate goal is control. As we have seen in previous chapters, it starts with control of operatives, but leads rapidly to the desire to control events, to control circumstances, and ultimately to be able to manipulate the very flow of history. The fantasy is an understandable one among the players in the spy v. spy world where no one can be trusted, nothing is what it appears, and truth is a relative thing, very much in the eye and mind of the beholder. Counter-intelligence is a world where uncertainty and anxiety—not to say paranoia—are tools of the trade. Eventually, the idea of complete control has to become very seductive.

Wouldn't the world be a better place if the wars, revolutions, and inconvenient social movements could simply be eliminated by having the ability to instruct the population what to think and how to behave? In other words, wouldn't it be a whole lot better simply to reshape

THE IDEA OF THE PSYCHO-CIVILIZED SOCIETY

global society in a way that would make it much more manageable? And where better to start such management than at the very core of the problem? If human minds can be controlled, then all else should logically follow from this.

Unfortunately, what would logically follow would be the most absolute form of totalitarianism imaginable, with a small hidden power elite controlling a human anthill completely unable to think for itself. The psycho-civilized society would be, like they used to say in those 1950s black and white horror movies, "the end of civilization as we know it." Humanity may be a quarrelsome, overpopulating mess, here at the dawn of the 21st century, but it is, at least, our very own mess, and not a mindless quasi-utopia where every aspect of life would be planned out for us by the director of the CIA or some other shadowy dictator. We will either solve our current problems or we won't. What the human race doesn't need is for the ability to solve problems—and, on the other side of the coin, to screw up fully—to be nullified by men, women, and children being uniformly drugged, wired, implanted, or bombarded with microwaves.

Regrettably, small but determined groups of men and women still don't agree with the preceding statement and apparently continue to work toward the goal of control as though it was the cure for all our ills, and at least one of those groups is almost certainly deep inside the most secret power corridors of the Central Intelligence Agency.

Each time the media, the US Congress, or various watchdog and oversight bodies have attempted to investigate the involvement of the CIA and other intelligence agencies in mind control and related fields of research, the cover story has always been: "Yes, there was investigation of that kind of thing, but then the Agency realized that, if pursued, mind control and behavioral experiments might move into areas that were both morally and legally indefensible, and thus were terminated." When MKULTRA was broken up in 1963, the impression was given that the LSD and hypnosis experiments were a mistake that had been rectified, and were a thing of the past. Again, in the 1970s, when the Rockefeller Commission uncovered Stephen Aldrich's brain stimulation work with ORD, the same defense was offered: "Yes, we may have gone a little too far, but it won't happen again."

The mind experiments continue

As John Marks categorically proved, these statements were little short of deliberate deception and, after a period of laying low, the mind controllers continued on their merry way as though nothing had happened, funded by the

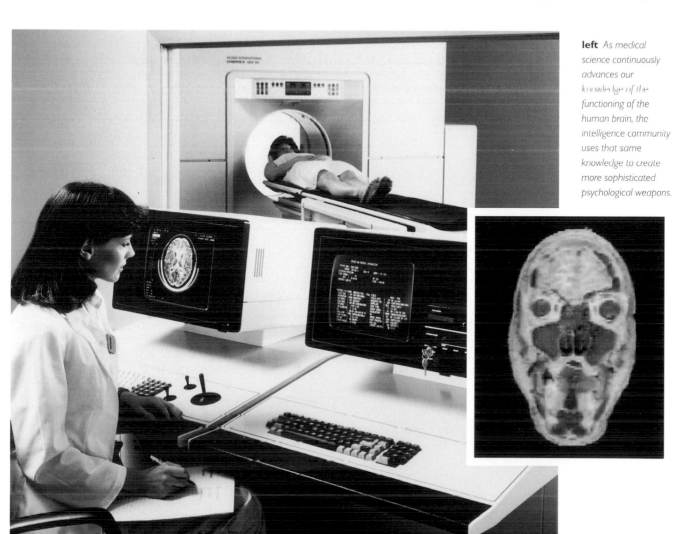

left *As medical science continuously advances our knowledge of the functioning of the human brain, the intelligence community uses that same knowledge to create more sophisticated psychological weapons.*

completely unaware US taxpayer. Since the early 1980s, literally dozens of pieces of information have floated to the surface, indicating that the Company's mind control ambitions are still alive and kicking. One of the first of these came from a former FBI agent, Lincoln Lawrence, who revealed the existence of a 350-page CIA document outlining a technique with the convoluted acronym RHIC-EDOM—Radio Hypnosis Intra-Cerebral Control—Electronic Dissolution of Memory. RHIC-EDOM would appear to be either an evolution or outgrowth of the ORD implant experiments, and the parallel ones by Dr. Jose Delgardo, who demonstrated a "stimoceiver" that "could excite extreme emotions—rage, lust, fatigue, etc." The apparent leap forward made by RHIC-EDOM was that, instead of hardwiring the actual brain, the same effects of disorientation and loss of memory could be achieved by various forms of electronic bombardment by radio and microwaves. Originally all of this work had been motivated by the long-term quest for the Manchurian Candidate assassin, but, as time passed, it began to be increasingly focused on methods of citizen control.

More documents came to light under the Freedom of Information Act that referred to another project, codenamed PANDORA, whose purpose was to "study the health and psychological effects of low intensity microwaves" with particular reference to the possibility of creating "auditory hallucinations," similar to the voices that many paranoid schizophrenics are convinced they hear in their heads and often interpret as the voice of God giving them instructions. In 1989, a CNN report revealed similar documents that indicated plans to field test various forms of electro-magnetic (EM) weapons for use against "terrorists," and that such weapons may have been loaned to either MOSSAD or the Israeli Army to use against rioting Palestinians.

One of the techniques described is that of "acoustic

left and below

Rioting Palestinians on the Left Bank of the Jordan may have been subjected to mind altering microwave transmissions, generated by either MOSSAD or the Israeli Army and allegedly supplied by the CIA. If this did happen, it hardly had the effect of making the subjects any more docile.

left *Anti-war protesters at England's Greenham Common may have been the subject of microwave weapons, and considered an ideal test bed for future actions against other political dissenters.*

below *The Branch Davidian compound at Waco, Texas, burns after the assault by FBI tanks and helicopters. Microwave weapons were allegedly deployed but not used.*

A DEVICE THAT COULD IMPLANT THOUGHTS IN PEOPLE

psycho-correction," the "transmission of specific commands via the static or white noise bands in the human subconscious." Known as the "Frey Effect," after its discoverer, Alan Frey, such transmissions can create a form of "microwave hearing, a form of artificial telepathy," or to put it another way, another version of the "voice of God," in the subject's head. Further confirmation of this kind of work was provided by ex-US Army Major Edward Dames, who had worked for a PANDORA-related psy-tech project, know as GRILL FLAME. On an NBC News prime-time TV special, "The Other Side," broadcast in April of 1995, Dames stated that "the US Government has an electronic device which could implant thoughts in people" and that the CIA was now working with various sections of law enforcement with a view to it being utilized in situations of "civil unrest, disobedience, and inner city turmoil created by an increasingly impoverished lower class."

The implication in this would seem to be that EM weapons have yet to be used in a real confrontation situation, but this again may not be the case. When in the 1980s, various women's peace groups set up camp around the USAF air base at Greenham Common in England to protest the presence of American nuclear weapons on British soil, reports started to come in of protesters suffering from a range of unexplainable symptoms, including "vertigo, retinal bleeding, burnt face, nausea, sleep disturbance, palpitations, loss of concentration and memory, and a sense of panic." In the opinion of Nobel Prize nominee, Dr. Robert Becker, all of these effects could have been created if the protesters were being regularly hosed down with low level EM emissions in an attempt to break their spirit and disrupt their sense of purpose and solidarity. Rumors also persist that EM weaponry was brought up by the FBI at the siege of the Branch Davidian

108

left *The HAARP facility at Gakona, Alaska. An atmospheric research project or more mind control?*

Compound outside of Waco, Texas, but in the end was never put to use against David Koresh and his followers.

Exciting the ionosphere

When electro-magnetic fields and microwaves became the CIA flavor of the moment, a project in the wilds of Alaska known as HAARP, almost unmentioned in the media aside from a small segment on *Sightings*, the TV series devoted to news of the paranormal, suddenly starts to demand our attention. HAARP, the acronym for High Frequency Active Aurora Research Program, is an installation in South Central Alaska, on the Tok Highway near the village of Gakona. The facility, ostensibly a joint venture between the US Army and Air Force, appears harmless enough from the outside. To the casual observer—and the site is not particularly well protected and reasonably accessible—it seems to be little more than a fairly extensive collection of radio masts. The HAARP project has its own website that plainly states the purpose of HAARP to be "studying the properties and behavior of the ionosphere." The web introduction continues: "the ionosphere instrument is a high powered transmitter operating in the HF frequency range that will be used to excite a limited area of the ionosphere for scientific study."

The first and very obvious question asked by the majority of HAARP critics, of which there are many—ranging from the academic to the highly paranoid—is: "Since when did the army and air force get into the business of peaceful scientific research, and if HAARP is not a weapon, what are they doing there? Surely, if the operation was pure geophysical high atmosphere research, why wouldn't it be operating under the auspices of NASA or a college like MIT or Stanford?"

Even the idea of "exciting" a section of the ionosphere fills many scientists with extreme misgivings. They point out that any high intensity EM pulse directed at the upper atmosphere threatens the natural atmospheric shields like the ozone layer, that reduces the ultraviolet content of sunlight, and the Van Allen Radiation Belts, that protect the Earth from hard cosmic radiation. Very little is known about the ionosphere and the idea of bombarding it with HF

transmissions is the scientific equivalent of hitting it with a hammer to see if it breaks. Critics warn that the possible repercussions could be the jamming of international communications, the endangerment of commercial airline traffic, and even a serious disruption of global weather patterns. Even before HAARP was fully powered up, nearby residents in the surrounding countryside were already complaining about interference with their TV reception.

The fact that the military is involved in the project provokes considerable suspicion that the real purpose of HAARP is to discover if these predicted disruptions could be created and controlled as weapons. A nation that can influence the weather or shut down radio and radar transmission at will wields an incredible power over its neighbors. Along with this suspicion comes a high degree of anxiety that the army and air force will show no more sensitivity to the possible long-term effects of what they're doing with HAARP than they did during the nuclear weapon testing of the 1940s, '50s, and '60s. The cancer rates alone among the soldiers who participated in the Nevada A-bomb

A COVER FOR A NEW GROUND-BASED PHASE OF STAR WARS

tests were of frightening proportions. If HAARP was to do its worst, we could find ourselves looking at a global disaster of the most awesome proportions. A number of HAARP critics take this a stage further and state that the advertised ionosphere research is nothing more than a cover for a new ground-based phase of the Reagan era Strategic Defense Initiative (SDI)—the Star Wars program.

Dr. Nicholas Beglich is one of the most vociferous critics of HAARP and has been actively monitoring HAARP transmissions. He claims that his research has revealed a group of emissions in the 435 MHz range. He reasons that, since the window frequency of human consciousness is supposedly in the area of 400–450 MHz, some of HAARP's

left *"ET Highway" near Nevada's mysterious Area 51. One CIA psychic is reputed to have inadvertently penetrated the super-secret base, the home of various "stealth projects" and, according to some theorists, where the captured alien spacecraft are tested.*

WAS A "PSYCHIC GAP" BEING CREATED BETWEEN EAST AND WEST

more covert objectives are actually in the realm of mind control. Which is, of course, where the CIA comes in. Dr. Beglich speculates that one of the uses of HAARP is to project the kind of EM transmissions developed by projects like PANDORA and GRILL FLAME, but on a mass scale. These signals of 400–450 MHz are seemingly capable of resonating neutrons in the human brain and directly affecting the mental processes. Briefly, the scenario he postulates is roughly as follows. The HAARP broadcasts could be bounced back to Earth via the small SDI "popcorn" satellites that have been in orbit since the late 1980s and the effects recorded as a preliminary research into the ultimate possibility of creating that longed-for psycho-civilized society.

The idea may seem fanciful in the extreme, but the kicker in the whole HAARP controversy is—as with so many CIA adventures in the human mind—that we won't know anything about it until it is much too late.

Remote viewing

The possibilities of the HAARP project may seem to verge on the fantastic, but in comparison to Company research into the paranormal and, particularly, the well-documented experiments in what is known as "remote viewing," they start to look positively mundane. As with so many other pieces of Cold War weirdness, the move into the supernatural by the Pentagon and the CIA started with the perception that the Soviets might have an edge in the paranormal field, that maybe the Reds knew more than they did. Was a "psychic gap" being created in the face-off between East and West, just like the "bomber gap" and the "missile gap" that had both been used in the 1950s and 1960s to crank up defense spending? Records indicate that the problem was discussed at the highest level. Through the 1950s and 1960s rumors repeatedly circulated that the Russians had secret installations where men and women sat in soundproofed, underground bunkers attempting to read each other's thoughts and move billiard balls with their minds. The army and the CIA began work on an exploratory project to see if there was any way that the unexplained and supernatural could be turned to a military or intelligence gathering advantage.

It wasn't until the US Army began tentative exploration into the phenomenon of "remote viewing" that the

THE CIA IN CYBERSPACE

It would seem that, on the highly promoted "information superhighway," the CIA already has its radar, hidden cameras, and "cyber-highway patrol" in place. At a hearing of the of the Senate Sub-Committee on Government Affairs in June 1996, CIA Director John Deutch attempted to alarm committee members with the potential threat to national security posed by both amateur hackers and computer terrorists working for hostile governments. "The electron is the ultimate precision guided weapon," Deutch told the committee. "We have evidence that a number of countries around the world are developing the doctrine strategies and tools to conduct information attacks." When asked by Senator Sam Nunn of Georgia whether the CIA was seriously expecting some kind of "electronic Pearl Harbor," Deutch did his best to sound as ominous as possible. "I'm certainly prepared to predict some very, very large and uncomfortable incidents."

Deutch went on to explain that cyber attacks would not be merely confined to government computer systems, but that industrial targets and private corporations could also be included in any coordinated cyber blitz on the USA. Banks, hospitals, and even air traffic control systems could all find themselves vulnerable to this kind of electronic terrorism.

Although Deutch produced figures from the US General Accounting Office that showed, in 1995 alone, over 250,000 intrusion attempts had been made on US military computers, and stated that these numbers more than justified CIA plans to set up its own Information Warfare Technology Center, many commentators saw the CIA presentation as yet another attempt by the Agency to justify its continued existence in the post-Cold War world.

Whether seriously concerned or simply looking for a supposed threat to justify itself, the Company certainly has become a major presence in cyberspace. A recent report by the Civil Liberties Committee of the European Parliament revealed that the CIA, working in concert with the National Security Agency and British intelligence operations, routinely intercept phone, fax, and e-mail transmissions all over the world. The same report revealed the existence of ECHELON, a part of the Anglo-American UKUSA system of supercomputers through which monitored transmissions are collected at a central hub in London and then sent by satellite to Fort Meade in Maryland via the Menwith Hill facility in Yorkshire, now the biggest spy station in the world. Unlike the older electronic spy systems developed during the Cold War that eavesdropped on purely military communications, ECHELON targets civilian governments, organizations, and businesses in virtually every country. "The system works by indiscriminately intercepting very large quantities of communications and then siphoning out what is valuable by using artificial intelligence aids like MEMEX to find key words."

The report concludes by bluntly advising: "The European Parliament should reject proposals from the United States to have private messages on the global communications network (the internet) accessible to US intelligence agencies."

111

112

existence of a Soviet psychic unit was supposedly confirmed. Remote viewing, an unexplained latent ability in some individuals—not unlike telepathy—is to be able to sense and describe both people and objects at distances of 1000 miles or more without ever physically having seen them. Those who appear to have this gift of what was once called clairvoyance, precognition, or second sight are as much at a loss to explain exactly how it works as the scientists who have studied them. They talk in terms of clearing their minds and letting the images come. Although it seems primarily to be a quasi-visual sense, it would also appear to be random, imprecise, and hard to control.

Much of the early psychic experimentation is as cloaked in mystery as anything that went on at ORD or MKULTRA, but the incident that is reputed to have triggered the establishment of a full-time psychic spy unit seemingly occurred during remote viewing research being conducted at the Stanford Research Institute, an academic body that has cooperated with the CIA on a variety of projects. Under the supervision of Project Director Dale Graff, a Stanford remote viewer attempted to psychically search out any possible Soviet paranormal research centers. The operative had the distinct impression that he was making positive headway when he suddenly perceived what he could only assume was a Russian remote viewer "looking" right back at him. This freakish Cold War confrontation was more than enough to motivate Major General Edmund R. Thompson to set up a combined army, air force, and CIA permanent psychic spy unit at Fort Meade that operated under the codename STARGATE.

STARGATE

The STARGATE unit's work was still basically experimental but, little by little, they were increasingly called in to consult on actual field operations. One of the first of these calls was after a highly secret Russian TU22 fighter-bomber went down somewhere in the interior of Zaire in Central Africa. Both the CIA and the air force urgently wanted to get their hands on the wreckage, but agents on the ground couldn't locate the crash site. It was apparently at this point that STARGATE was let loose on the problem.

STARGATE REMOTE VIEWERS HAD BEEN LOANED OUT

With much the same reservation and reluctance displayed by police detectives who bring in a psychic when a homicide investigation seems to be going nowhere by conventional means, the air force asked remote viewers at Fort Meade to try and find the Soviet aircraft. This search for the crashed TU22 was confirmed years later by no less than ex-President Jimmy Carter, who recounted the story of how a female psychic unit member provided satellite coordinates for the wreckage that enabled a covert team to go in the African bush and come out with an intelligence treasure trove of state-of-the-art enemy technology. "She told us where to look, we looked there, and there it was."

Following the TU22 success, the STARGATE remote viewers were called in on other missions. They attempted to locate hostages in Lebanon and Iran, they psychically hunted down the Russian Typhoon-class super submarine, and in 1979 they gave warning of the misfire of a Chinese underground nuclear weapon test. Recently declassified documents reveal that STARGATE sent 183 confidential reports to the Joint Chiefs of Staff, including a prediction of the Iranian rocket attack on the USS *Starke*, the results of attempts to locate US Army General William Dozier after his kidnapping by the Italian Red Brigades, and of their participation in the hunt for Carlos the Jackal. At one point STARGATE even attempted to find MIA prisoners who might still be held in Vietnam. It was also rumored that STARGATE remote viewers had been loaned out to the coast guard, US Customs, and the DEA, in attempts to aid narcotics interception, creating yet another of those uncomfortable and constitutionally forbidden liaisons between the CIA and domestic law enforcement.

Even though it may, at times, have been sailing close to the legal wind, STARGATE seemed to be making progress and justifying its existence. This progress, however, was not achieved without both problems and a considerable adverse response from more traditionalist sections of the military. One of the first problems noticed by the men and women of STARGATE was that remote viewing could produce odd aftereffects. A detached dreaminess seemed to take over for a number of hours after a remote viewing session. Sometimes that dreaminess could go as far as

113

left *A Chinese nuclear test site photographed by a US spy satellite. Part of STARGATE's task was to tell satellite controllers where to point their cameras.*

Ground Zero

right *Carlos the Jackal and his personal armory. (All the weapons shown were in a bag discarded after his 1975 killing of a Lebanese counter intelligence operative and two French agents.). The STARGATE program attempted to track him down*

★
114
=

strange and irrational acts. Melvin C. Riley, a former Army Master Sergeant who had been recruited after showing an almost uncanny skill in photo analysis during his tour in Vietnam, tells how, on one occasion, he walked out of a remote viewing session and, for no apparent reason, tossed his car keys into a nearby dumpster.

Other bizarre incidents occurred during the actual sessions. When a STARGATE team were given the mission of discovering the secrets of Soviet experimental aircraft, one remote viewer found that, again and again, he was drawing images of a strange, bat-like craft with wide, geometric, indented wings and a strange, vestigial, V-shaped tail. The drawings were routinely taken away and he heard no more about them. (One of the major complaints from the STARGATE operatives was that they were never allowed to know the results of their work.) It was only years later that he discovered the craft that he'd

"I WOULDN'T BELIEVE THIS EVEN IF IT WAS TRUE"

been drawing was the US Stealth bomber. Instead of penetrating Russian airfields, the operative had somehow been turned around and psychically surfaced inside the ultra-secret Nevada installation know as Area 51.

The problems that beset STARGATE were not just directional, physical, and psychological. Its very existence split the Pentagon and the CIA into two opposing camps. On one side was the view that messing around with the paranormal was the greatest example of CIA foolishness ever created at Langley. One top government scientist flatly stated: "I wouldn't believe this even if it was true." Many on the military side also felt that the technique was too hit and miss to be of any real use, and that its successes were little more than coincidences or fortuitous lucky breaks. Since remote viewing couldn't be explained scientifically, it also couldn't be trusted in practical application. A powerful group within the Pentagon, led by General Ed Soyster, lobbied to have the project cancelled. Although a career army man, Edmund Thompson, STARGATE's founder and

right *The ultra-secret F-117 Stealth fighter-bomber. When a STARGATE remote viewer produced drawings of the aircraft, many high-ranking officers at the Pentagon became uncomfortable about the CIA's use of psychics and pressure built to cancel the program.*

patron, took the exact opposite view of the operation's usefulness. "I didn't want to explain it. I just wanted to find out if it could be used operationally."

Head of STARGATE research, Frederick Atwater, adopted a similar position. Remote viewing could never be an end in itself or a complete source of data. It had to be looked on as just one of "multiple sources of cross verification, an investigative aid." Many in the CIA went along with Thompson and Atwater. They were far more accustomed to dealing with random pieces of a puzzle— superficially unrelated bits of data that needed to be cross-referenced and cross-verified. The spooks could see beyond the military need to have everything neat, complete, and squared away, and they were happy to let the remote viewers of STARGATE keep doing their thing. The controversy raged on until early in 1995, when the US Congress moved into the picture and ordered an independent investigation of STARGATE. Even the investigators couldn't agree on the actual or potential value of the project, and in the end it was money that had the final word. The idea that over $20 million had been spent on paranormal spying was too much for vote-conscious

senators and congressman, and STARGATE was unceremoniously scrapped in November 1995.

Jessica Utts, one of the panel of STARGATE investigators, feels that the all-too-rapid cancellation of the project was a serious error: "I believe the government made a mistake in pulling the rug out from under remote viewing. It would have been better to move it into the open scientific field and investigate it properly." Utts' statement reinforces the constant complaint by the operatives themselves, that STARGATE and the remote viewing phenomenon was kept needlessly secret. One operative commented wryly: "There was too much of a giggle factor. Much of the secrecy that surrounded the program was more to protect its supporters from embarrassment than to preserve national security."

For once, it seemed, the CIA was concerned about its image. Seemingly, the Company felt that to be seen to be in the paranormal research business made it look too much like a mad confederacy of kooks and crackpots. The irony in this is, to say the least, hard to miss. STARGATE was, without a doubt, one of the Agency's more benign and innocuous secret programs. As far as can be ascertained,

THE CIA AT THE MOVIES

Nowhere is the changing public perception of the Central Intelligence Agency more easily demonstrated than by the way that it's been treated by moviemakers and thriller writers. In the early days of the Company, the imagination of the pop culture world was totally captured by Ian Fleming and the James Bond phenomenon. American efforts at "Bondage," like Dean Martin as Matt Helm or James Coburn as Our Man Flint, took a very distant back seat to the all-prevailing 007. In a number of Bond novels and movies, however, the CIA man Felix Leiter does make an appearance, and the overall picture of the Company is one of a slick, high-tech operation that may not be totally trustworthy, but is all that stands between democracy and the communist hordes. This concept was cheerfully reinforced on TV by Robert Culp and Bill Cosby in *I-Spy*.

Gradually, however, the picture began to change. Although the British still made the spy movie, running with films like *The Spy Who Came in from the Cold* and *The Ipcress File*, the CIA started to be seen as one more player in the rather squalid but unavoidable game of counter-espionage. By the latter half of the 1960s and on into the 1970s, films like *The Naked Runner*, starring the late Frank Sinatra, and Robert Redford's *Three Days of the Condor*, painted an even more grim picture of the Agency as a dangerous and duplicitous organization, often locked into its own private and deadly agendas. Throughout the Reagan 1980s—as, under the management of William Colby, the CIA enjoyed a renaissance of deceit and covert ops—it also took a hammering from Hollywood with films like *Apocalypse Now, Missing, The Falcon and the Snowman,* and Oliver Stone's *Salvador,* all of which made it appear that the Company was one of the primary sources of evil in the world.

In the 1990s, the perception was softened a little, particularly by the movies and best sellers of Tom Clancy. Clancy's hero, Jack Ryan, is portrayed as the lone honest man doing the best he can in a corrupt and desperate world, although, in *A Clear and Present Danger*, one of the villains of the piece does turn out to be the President of the United States.

116

left *"You are an errand boy sent by grocery clerks..."*

THE HEART OF DARKNESS

no one died, no one went insane, and no governments were overthrown. In 1995, the CIA had far more serious problems of image and public perception.

If one had to identify the CIA's greatest failure over the course of its half century of life, it has to be in the field of the most basic public relations. Until the world becomes a utopia of peace and plenty, nations will have a need for spies and intelligence gathering organizations, and part of the function of government will be the protection of its citizens from possible outside enemies. On the principle that forewarned is forearmed, the job of the intelligence agency has to be to identify those enemies, ideally before they can pose too dangerous a threat. No one can reasonably expect a country's spies to wear kid gloves at all times. Spying is, by definition, a dirty business, but someone has to do it. In the same way, no one seriously requires an operation like the Central Intelligence Agency to put on a happy face for the public as though it was a manufacturer of breakfast cereals or detergent, or that it should make public all of its inner workings and hard won secrets. The very foundation of successful spying has to be not to let the enemy know what you know, unless it is to gain an advantage.

THE CIA SHOULD NOT EXPECT TO BE LIKED

Reassessing and redefining

The CIA should not expect to be liked. No one is happy to see a police car appear in his or her rear view mirror, but, at the same time, the majority of the population recognize that the policeman is a needed factor in society. The CIA, on the other hand, does not even seem to enjoy that level of public trust and confidence. When an admittedly partisan writer on the "Sightings" website can refer to "the CIA snake crawling through banana republics causing poverty, urban unrest, famine, civil wars" or journalist Gary Webb can connect the Agency with the sale of crack cocaine on the streets of South Central Los Angeles, the fact has to be faced—if something is not deeply and fundamentally wrong within the Agency itself, at the very least, something is seriously off track with the public perception of it. So off track, in fact, that, way over on the outer limits, fear of the agency has become a psychosis. Jim Jones was firmly convinced that the CIA was out to get him, as were the

suicidal members of the Heaven's Gate cult.

Defenders of the Company will dismiss many of the charges made against it as the fantasies of extremists of either the left or the right. The CIA cannot be held responsible for the fact that a few lunatics have made it a part of their delusional world. Other crazies are just as upset by the IRS, Microsoft, the phone company, or even the neighbor's cat or their own domestic TV set. Where the CIA is concerned, however, obsession seems to know no bounds.

Ex-Office of Naval Intelligence Agent William Cooper, in his book *Behold a Pale Horse*, charges that not only is the CIA fully under the control of the international New World Order, but also in cahoots with aliens from outer space. He goes on to lay out the theory that this three-way combination is planning a totalitarian takeover of the entire world during the confusion created by the millennium. Confronted by this kind of weirdness, anyone could be justified in dismissing Cooper and those like him as either crazy or charlatans preying on public paranoia and ignorance. Unfortunately, at the beginning of the Frank Olson cover-up, the hapless LSD victim was also called crazy. The first rumors to circulate about Sidney Gottlieb and his work at MKULTRA were dismissed as paranoia, and when New Orleans District Attorney Jim Garrison attempted to link certain CIA operatives and ex-agents with the Kennedy assassination, his sanity was also called into question. When accusations of madness are the first fallback position of what the Agency calls "plausible deniability", it only strengthens the case of someone like Bill Cooper.

The CIA today finds itself in the position of the little boy who cried "Wolf!" Not only the people of the United States, but the population of the world at large, has been lied to too many times already to take a statement by a CIA director or any of his underlings at face value. The Agency has attempted to scare us with so many horror stories and tales of Reds under the bed that we now think twice about believing their warnings, valid or otherwise. In the 1960s we were told that, if Vietnam fell to the communists, India would be the next to go. Vietnam became a communist state in the mid-1970s but, more than 20 years later, India is still a democracy—admittedly a ramshackle democracy—but a democracy all the same. Later we were

★

117

left *The U2 spyplane; the CIA denied the U2 was making flights into Soviet airspace until the Russians shot one down. They also denied that Lee Harvey Oswald worked on the base in Japan where these flights originated.*

below *The bodies of Heaven's Gate cultists are removed from their California home. CIA paranoia would seem to have been a contributory factor in their 1997 mass suicide.*

told to expect the Sandinistas to be rolling across the Texas border in Soviet-built tanks if they were ever to come to power in Nicaragua. The Sandinistas came to power and, after years of CIA covert attempts at destabilization and sabotage, they were voted out of office in a conventional election. Texas, meanwhile, has remained pretty much as it always was. Thus when current CIA Director John Deutch tells us that he needs to have access to our personal e–mail and records of our online purchases to protect us from cyber terrorists, we tend to think long and hard before believing him.

Over the years, the public has heard too many CIA denials that have later been disproved by the course of history. The Company claimed it had no connection with Lee Oswald until confronted by his CIA character profile. The Company denied spy flights were being made over Soviet airspace until Russian missiles brought down Francis Gary Powers in his U2 spyplane. They refuted allegations that they spied and maintained files on the activities of US citizens inside the United States—after all, wasn't that specifically prohibited by the terms of their founding charter—until Seymour Hersh revealed in the *New York Times* that the Agency had been doing exactly that during both the Johnson and Nixon administrations. It logically follows that the CIA would obviously deny it was cutting deals and making secret treaties with extra-terrestrials, whether it was or not. Maybe the idea is fantastic, but they have denied so much else and subsequently been caught in the lie that, for a single crucial moment, we stop and wonder. Could it just be possible? Of course not, but it's that instant of doubt that counts. The fact that a vast majority of people routinely question any statement made by the Agency has the unpleasant side effect that it lends a certain measure of unwarranted credence to some of the most far-fetched and paranoid stories about its operations and objectives.

In all fairness, the majority of CIA employees do not

THE GREAT AIDS RUMOR

Perhaps the greatest gauge of the distrust of the CIA among large sections of the world's population is the perpetuation of the rumor that the CIA, working with the NSA and the Army Chemical Corps Special Operations Division (the notorious SOD) at Fort Detrick, Maryland, designed, developed, and then set loose the HIV virus on an unsuspecting planet. For over a decade, the tale of the Agency being responsible for the AIDS epidemic has circulated among black activists, gay militants, and conspiracy buffs. The author of this book profoundly hopes that, in actuality, there is no truth in the story. If there was, it would certainly qualify as the worst and most evil atrocity in world history, eclipsing even that of the Nazi death camps, and would certainly be enough reason, quite on its own, as John Kennedy once put it, to "tear down the Agency, brick by brick."

At the core of this AIDS hypothesis is an alleged budget appropriation, passed by the US Congress in 1969 as part of House Bill 15090. HB 15090 apparently included $10 million for, as subsequent Senate Committee testimony is supposed to have revealed, the production of "a synthetic biological agent for which no natural immunity could have been acquired...a new infective microorganism which could differ in certain important aspects from any known disease-carrying organisms. Most important of these is that it might be refractory to the immunological and therapeutic processes upon which we depend to maintain our relative freedom from infectious disease."

The development of this bacterial weapon that could plainly do nothing except create a prolonged and deadly pandemic was to be part of a CIA subgroup known as MKNAOMI, one of the offspring operations that followed in the tracks of MKULTRA.

How the scenario unfolds

Since no hard evidence seems to exist beyond this point, the speculation takes off from there. The ultimate use of the bacteria was virtually to depopulate the continent of Africa, leaving its vast land area and underlying natural resources open for exploitation by western corporations. Initially, however, the field tests of the man-made and sexually-transmitted epidemic were to be made on "undesirable sections of the domestic population"—blacks, gays, and Hispanics were specifically targeted. The US testing was carried out by agents working under the cover of a hepatitis B research program, supposedly conducted at the Center for Disease Control, in New York, San Francisco, and four other US cities. Once these were complete, the virus was introduced into Africa by a smallpox immunization program operated by the World Health Organization.

Again, at this point, we have to make it clear that no satisfactory hard evidence can be produced linking AIDS to a global CIA conspiracy, and we only mention it here as an indication of the total distrust the Agency seems to have managed to engender. The fact does remain, however, that AIDS is currently ravaging Africa and, to quote epidemic specialist Dr. Robert Strecker, "without a cure, the entire black population of Africa will be dead within 15 years. Some countries are beyond epidemic status."

119

THE TALE OF THE AGENCY BEING RESPONSIBLE FOR THE AIDS EPIDEMIC

carry weapons and wear shoulder holsters; they do not implant electrodes in human brains; they do not destabilize foreign countries and do not plan the assassinations of presidents. The majority of CIA employees sit at desks, they shuffle papers, they stare into computer screens, and attempt to index, file and cross-reference the mountains of raw data that flow into Langley and the other agency centers, hour by hour and day after day. They read books, magazines, and newspapers from all over the world and in all languages, and attempt to make sense and discover items of significance in this endless river of trivia. This is the normal work of intelligence gathering. The MKULTRAs, the ORDs, the STARGATEs that we've dealt with here are the work of a comparatively small number of the Company's agents who have gone far beyond that comfortable norm of data gathering and processing.

When he ran for president in 1964 against Lyndon Johnson, Senator Barry Goldwater made the bold statement that "an excess of zeal in the defense of

"IT'S A DIRTY JOB BUT SOMEONE HAS TO OVERDO IT"

freedom is no crime." For some sections of the CIA—unfortunately quite often in the uppermost echelons of the Agency—that creed has been taken to almost absurd extremes. For the CIA, at its worst, excess was something without tangible limits, almost as though they had rewritten the well-known saying so it now read: "It's a dirty job, but someone has to overdo it." For most of its 50-year life, the CIA has had the excuse that communism was an overwhelming threat to the free world and, in combating that threat, no action could be deemed beyond acceptable limits. If, in the battle for freedom, thousands have to lose their liberty or even their lives, so be it. If America is to be saved from the scourge of drugs by the CIA becoming one of the biggest players in the international narcotics trade, live with it. The means will always justify the end.

above *Sen. Daniel Patrick Moynihan has called for the dismantling of the CIA.*

right *CIA Director John Deutch attempts to convince citizens in South Central Los Angeles that the CIA wasn't responsible for the spread of crack cocaine through their community as part of a spin off from its covert operations in Central America.*

★
120
=

left *CIA headquarters in Langley, Virginia, photographed by one of its own spy satellites. Does the company have a future in the 21st century?*

Dismantling the CIA

Now the Red Menace is gone, or at least confined to the impoverished island of Cuba, and the Company can no longer excuse its more extreme methods of doing business by claims of being engaged in a death struggle with a mortal enemy and a fundamentally evil ideology, many critics of the CIA have again rewritten the old slogan. The version for the 1990s has read. "It's a dirty job, but does anyone have to do it?" Among others, New York Senator Daniel Patrick Moynihan has pointed out that advanced computers, and spy satellite technology that can photograph areas of a few square yards from high orbit, has made the covert ops, the games of spy v. spy, and all the weird secret research, redundant and possibly dangerous to the world's real security. Moynihan has repeatedly called for the reform or dismantling of the Agency, while, for the other side, Director Deutch and the CIA's political supporters attempt to make a case to preserve the Agency as a bastion against terrorism, drugs, cyberwar, nuclear proliferation, or any other replacement threat they can substitute for Soviet aggression.

A third—and maybe the most chilling—point of view is that it might not in fact be possible to dismantle the Agency. Like the Hydra of Greek myth, you cut off the head and ten more grow in its place. A Central Intelligence Agency with at least tenuous ties to a governing body might be better than an armed and dangerous, totally uncontrolled, multifaceted global information cartel with connections at all levels, and responsibility to no one. In the end, the only way to close down the CIA would be to revoke its charter and cut off its money. Whether this can be done is highly debatable. For years the CIA has received funding from "black" defense budgets, hundreds of millions of dollars, all without the slightest congressional oversight. In addition, it actually makes its own money, from investments in on-going enterprises that range from drug trafficking to the ownership of banks and airlines, and these may only be the tips of a financial iceberg. It is quite impossible to estimate the extent of the Agency's ties to some of the world's most powerful corporations and the support it might receive from them. It is not beyond either reason or possibility that, if pushed to it, the CIA, or some kind of immediate descendant, could actually stand alone as a vast, autonomous entity, operating either for hire or according to agendas of its own devising. Not for nothing is it known as "the Company."

INDEX

CREDITS AND ACKNOWLEDGMENTS

PICTURE CREDITS

Key: t = top; b = bottom; c = center; l = left; r = right

Associated Press: 70/71, 74 (tl)
The Fortean Picture Library: 59, 103 (cl)
Frank Spooner Pictures: 111
Her Majesty's Customs & Excise: 21 (t), 36 (bl)
The Hulton Getty Collection: 60 (tl, tr, bl), 64 (cl), 65, 69
The Kobal Collection: 20, 87, 94, 97, 101, 102 (br), 116
Popperfoto: 12, 13 (cl), 16, 17, 18, 21 (cr), 22, 23, 24, 25, 27, 30, 31 (tl), 32, 33 (cr), 37, 38, 40, 41, 42, 43, 44, 45, 46, 49, 53 (tr), 54, 55, 57, 58, 60 (br), 64 (br), 66, 67 (t), 72, 73 (cl), 74 (br), 75, 76, 77, 78 (br), 79 (cr), 80, 81 (cr), 82, 83 (cl), 84 (cl), 85 (br), 86, 88, 89, 90, 91 (cl, tc), 92, 95 (tr), 96 (tc, cl), 98, 99, 102 (tr, tl, bl), 103 (br), 104, 105 (br), 106, 107, 110, 114, 117, 118 (cr), 120
Private Collection: 35 (b), 63, 67 (cr), 68, 70, 74 (tr), 91 (tr), 100, 108, 113, 121
Quadrillion Publishing: 15, 31 (cr), 56
Rex Features: 50, 79 (tl), 81 (tl)
Robert Hunt Library: 19 (tc), 28, 61, 73 (t), 95 (cl)
Salamander Books: 39
TRH Pictures: 13 (br), 14, 19 (cr), 33 (t), 34, 35 (tr), 36 (c), 47, 52, 53 (tl), 78 (ct), 83 (br), 84 (tr), 85 (bl), 96 (tr), 105 (bl), 109, 112, 115, 118 (tc)

Editor
Simon Tuite

Design
Peter Laws

Design Manager
Justina Leitão

Picture Research
Tony Moore

Jacket Design
Mary Ryan/
Philip Chidlow

Production
Sandra Dixon
Janine Seddon

Director of Editorial
Will Steeds

Art Director
Philip Chidlow

Acknowledgments
Robin Haislip   Photo researcher and *femme fatale.*

Interrorgation, 1997, courtesy of ParaScope